MINISTRY IN COMMUNITY
RAHNER'S VISION OF MINISTRY

Louvain Theological and Pastoral Monographs is a publishing venture whose purpose is to provide those involved in pastoral ministry throughout the world with studies inspired by Louvain's long tradition of theological excellence within the Roman Catholic Tradition. The volumes selected for publication in the series are expected to express some of today's finest reflection on current theology and pastoral practice.

LOUVAIN THEOLOGICAL & PASTORAL MONOGRAPHS
—————————— 13 ——————————

MINISTRY IN COMMUNITY

RAHNER'S VISION OF MINISTRY

Jerry T. Farmer

PEETERS PRESS
LOUVAIN

W.B. EERDMANS

Cover Illustration by Leonce Verlinden-Vande Gucht.

ISBN 90-6831-507-2
D. 1993/0602/59

Contents

BIBLIOGRAPHY

PART ONE

RAHNER'S ECCLESIOLOGY

CHAPTER I

EARLY ECCLESIOLOGICAL REFLECTIONS

PART TWO

MINISTERIAL OFFICE

CHAPTER I

THE MEANING OF
THE ONE MINISTERIAL OFFICE

CHAPTER II

FURTHER SHARING
IN THE ONE MINISTERIAL OFFICE

Conclusion

BIBLIOGRAPHY

Comprehensive chronological bibliographies of the works of Karl Rahner have been published and are readily available. The four principal bibliographies that include all of his works are given in Section I of this bibliography. There is no need to repeat the work that has already been done.

Section II is a working bibliography. The complete reference for a work is given the first time that it is cited in the notes, and it is also found in the bibliography.

Often a short title is assigned to a particular work when it is referred to frequently. These short titles appear in the bibliography in bold print, and an entry is alphabetized according to its short title so that it may be readily consulted.

Section II is divided into three parts:

A. Works of Karl Rahner
B. Joint works of Karl Rahner and other authors
C. Works of other authors

It is important to note that a great majority of Rahner's theological writings were originally composed as separate articles or addresses. It is therefore misleading to refer first of all to a collection of Rahner's articles, such as one finds in Theological Investigations. Thus, reference is always made first to the name of the article, and then, if applicable, its location in a particular collection is noted. The significance of an article being incorporated into a collection is that it is recognized by Rahner to be of special import, judged to be of a certain enduring nature.

A technical consideration may be noted. In order to clearly distinguish between the German original and the corresponding English translation of multi-volume works, the English translation volumes are referred to by arabic numerals, and the volumes of the German original by roman numerals.

SECTION I

Bleistein, R., *Bibliographie Karl Rahner 1924-1969*, Freiburg, 1969.
Bleistein, R., *Bibliographie Karl Rahner 1969-1974*, Freiburg, 1974.
Imhof, P., Treziak, H., *Bibliographie Karl Rahner 1974-1979* in Vorgrimler, H. (ed.), *Wagnis Theologie*, Freiburg, 1979, pp. 579-597.
Imhof, P., Meuser, E., *Bibliographie Karl Rahner 1979-1984* in Klinger, E., Wittstadt, K. (eds.), *Glaube im Prozess*, Freiburg, 1984 (Second Edition), pp. 854-888.

SECTION II

1. Works of Karl Rahner

Rahner, K., *Basic Communities* in *TI*, Vol. 19, London, 1984, pp. 159-165; ET of: *ST*, Bd. XIV, Einsiedeln, 1980, pp. 265-272. (It was first presented as a lecture in Frankfurt 14 June 1975.)
Rahner, K., *Change*
Structural Change in the Church of the Future in *TI*, Vol. 20; London, 1981, pp. 115-132, esp. pp. 130-132; ET of: *ST*, Bd. XIV, Einsiedeln, 1980, pp. 333-354, esp. 352-354, first published in Braun, E. (ed.), *Gesellschaft als politischer Auftrag*, Graz, 1977, pp. 245-266.
Rahner, K., *Changeable and Unchangeable*
Basic Observations on the Subject of Changeable and Unchangeable Factors in the Church in *TI*, Vol. 14, London, 1976, pp. 3-23; ET of: *ST*, Bd. X, Einsiedeln, 1972, pp. 241-261; given as a lecture in 1970, first published in 1972.
Rahner, K., *Charismatic Observations*
Observations on the Factor of the Charismatic Church in *TI*, Vol. 12, London, 1974, pp. 81-97; ET of: *ST*, Bd. IX, Einsiedeln, 1970, pp. 415-431.
Rahner, K., *Church Future*
The Future of the Church and the Church of the Future in *TI*, Vol. 20, London, 1981, pp. 103-114; ET of: *ST*, Bd. XIV, Einsiedeln, 1980, pp. 319-332; originally given as a lecture 23 September 1977.
Rahner, K., *Church of Sinners*
The Church of Sinners in *TI*, Vol. 6, London, 1969, pp. 253-269; ET of: *ST*, Bd. VI, Einsiedeln, 1965, pp. 301-320. First published in *StdZ* 72 (1947) 163-177. (This article was the second of Rahner's writings to be published in ET, appearing in *Cross Currents* 3 (1951) 64-74.)
Rahner, K., *Church and World* in *SM*, Vol. 1, London, 1968, pp. 346-357; ET of: *SM*, Bd. II, Freiburg, 1968, cc. 1336-1357.

Rahner, K., *Church's Provenance*
The Church's Redemptive Historical Provenance for the Death and Resurrection of Jesus in *TI*, Vol. 19, London, 1984, pp. 24-38; ET of: *ST*, Bd. XIV, Einsiedeln, 1979, pp. 73-90; originally a lecture given 12 November 1976 in St. Pölten, and was first published in Reikerstorfer, J. (ed.), *Zeit des Geistes*, Vienna, 1977. (It was slightly revised by Rahner for the 1980 publication, Rahner, K., Thusing, W., *A New Christology*, pp. 18-30.)

Rahner, K., *Consecration*
Consecration in the Life and Reflection of the Church in *TI*, Vol. 19, London, 1984, pp. 57-72; ET of: *ST*, Bd. XIV, Einsiedeln, 1980, pp. 113-131; previously unpublished, but first given as a lecture 14 November 1976.

Rahner, K., *Courage*
Courage for an Ecclesial Christianity in *TI*, Vol. 20, London, 1981, pp. 3-12; ET of: *ST*, Bd. XIV, Einsiedeln, 1980, pp. 11-22; first published in Jens, W. (ed.), *Warum ich Christ bin*, Munich, 1979, pp. 296-309.

Rahner, K., *Departure*
The Point of Departure in Theology for Determining the Nature of the Priestly Office in *TI*, Vol. 12, London, 1974, pp. 31-38; ET of: *ST*, Bd. IX, Einsiedeln, 1970, pp. 366-382; first published in *Concilium* 43 (1969), pp. 80-86.

Rahner, K., *Development*
Theological Justification of the Church's Development Work in *TI*, Vol. 20, London, 1981, pp. 65-73; ET of: *ST*, Bd. XIV, Einsiedeln, 1980, pp. 273-283. This was first published in 1976 in a work edited by Bischöfliche Kommission für Misereor (ed.), *Miseror — Zeichen der Hoffnung* (*Festschrift Gottfried Dossing*), Munich, 1976, pp. 71-79.

Rahner, K., *Diaconate*
On the Diaconate in *TI*, Vol. 12, London, 1974, pp. 61-80; ET of: *ST*, Bd. IX, Einsiedeln, 1970, pp. 395-414; first given at a conference 7 December 1968 in Freiburg.

Rahner, K., *Dynamic Element*
The Dynamic Element in the Church (*QD*, 12), New York, 1964; ET of: *Das Dynamische in der Kirche* (*QD*, 5), Freiburg, 1958.

Rahner, K., *E Latere Christi*
E Latere Christi: Der Ursprung der Kirche als zweiter Eva aus der Seite Christi des Zweiten Adam. Eine Untersuchung über den typologischen Sinn von Jo 19,34, unpublished, 1936.

Rahner, K., *Epilogue* in Buhlmann, W., *The Church of the Future*, New York, 1986, pp. 185-197; ET of: Buhlmann, W., *Welt Kirche: Neue Dimensionen — Modell für das Jahr 2001*, Graz, 1984, pp. 220-234; first published in *Diakonia* 12 (1981) 221-235.

Rahner, K., *Episcopacy*

Pastoral-Theological Observations on Episcopacy in the Teaching of Vatican II in *TI*, Vol. 6, London, 1969, pp. 361-368; ET of: *ST*, Bd. VI, Einsiedeln, 1965, pp. 423-432; also published in *Concilium* 3 (1965), Glen Rock (New Jersey) pp. 15-23.

Rahner, K., *Episcopal Office*

The Episcopal Office in *TI*, Vol. 6, London, 1969, pp. 313-360; ET of: *ST*, Bd. VI, Einsiedeln, 1965, pp. 369-422; first published in *StdZ* 173 (1963/64) 161-195.

Rahner, K., *FCF*

Foundations of Christian Faith, London, 1978; ET of: *Grundkurs des Glaubens*, Freiburg, 1976.

Rahner, K., *Foundations*

Foundations of Christian Faith in *TI*, Vol. 19, London, 1984, pp. 3-15; ET of: *ST*, Bd. XIV, Einsiedeln, 1980, pp. 48-62. This was originally given as a lecture 28 February 1979, in Freiburg.

Rahner, K., *Humanization*

The Church's Commission to Bring Salvation and the Humanization of the World in *TI*, Vol. 14, London, 1976, pp. 295-313; ET of: *ST*, Bd. X, Einsiedeln, 1972, pp. 547-567. First presented as a lecture 13 October 1970 in Frankfurt, and first published in *GuL* 44 (1971) 32-48.

Rahner, K., *The Individual*

The Individual in the Church in Rahner, K., *Nature and Grace and other essays*, London, 1963, pp. 51-83; ET of: *Das Einzelne in der Kirche* in *StdZ* 139 (1946/1947) 260-276.

Rahner, K., *Meaning*

The Meaning of Ecclesiastical Office in Rahner, K., *SL*, London, 1968, pp. 13-45; ET of: Rahner, K., *Vom Sinn des kirchlichen Amtes*, Freiburg, 1966.

Rahner, K., *The Meaning of Frequent Confession of Devotion* in *TI*, Vol. 3, London, 1967, pp. 177-189; ET of: *ST*, Bd. III, Einsiedeln, 1959 (Third Edition), pp. 211-225; first published in *ZAM* 9 (1934) 323-336.

Rahner, K., *Membership*

Membership of the Church According to the Teaching of Pius XII's Encyclical 'Mystici Corporis Christi' in *TI*, Vol. 2, London, 1963, pp. 1-88; ET of: *ST*, Bd. II, Einsiedeln, 1955, pp. 7-94; first published in *ZKTh* 69 (1947) 129-160. (The version in *ST* is updated in regard to the notes.)

Rahner, K., *Methodology*

Reflections on Methodology in Theology in *TI*, Vol. 11, London, 1974, pp. 68-114; ET of: *ST*, Bd. IX, Einsiedeln, 1970, pp. 79-126. (The three lectures of 1969 appear as one essay in published form and had not been published before appearing in *ST*.)

Rahner, K., *Multiplication of Masses* in *Orate Fratres* 24 (1950) 553-562; ET of: Rahner, K., *Die vielen Messen und das eine Opfer*, Freiburg, 1951; first published in *ZKTh* 71 (1949) 257-317. (This is the first of Rahner's works to appear in ET.)

Rahner, K., *New Image*

The New Image of the Church in *TI*, Vol. 10, London, 1973, pp. 3-29; ET of: *ST*, Bd. VIII, Einsiedeln, 1967, pp. 329-354; first published in *GuL* 39 (1966) 4-24.

Rahner, K., *On the Divine Right of the Episcopate* in Rahner, K., Ratzinger, J., *EP*, Freiburg, 1962, pp. 64-135; ET of: Rahner, K., Ratzinger, J., *EuP*, Freiburg, 1961, pp. 60-125.

Rahner, K., *Open Questions*

Open Questions in Dogma Considered by the Institutional Church as Definitively Answered in *JES* 15 (1978) 211-226; ET of: *Scheinprobleme in der ökumenischen Diskussion* in *ST*, Bd. XIII, Einsiedeln, 1978; also translated in *TI*, Vol. 18, London, 1984, pp. 35-53.

Rahner, K., *Parousia*

The Church and the Parousia of Christ in *TI*, Vol. 6, London, 1969, pp. 295-312; ET of: *ST*, Bd. VI, Einsiedeln, 1965, pp. 348-367; first published in *Cath* 17 (1963) 113-128.

Rahner, K., *Pastoral Ministries*

Pastoral Ministries and Community Leadership in *TI*, Vol. 19, London, 1984, pp. 73-86; ET of: *ST*, Bd. XIV, Einsiedeln, 1980, pp. 132-147; first published in *StdZ* 195 (1977) 733-743.

Rahner, K., *Pierced Heart*

The Man with the Pierced Heart in *SL*, London, 1968, pp. 107-119; ET of: *KC*, Freiburg, 1967, pp. 117-133.

Rahner, K., *Pope and College*

On the Relationship between the Pope and the College of Bishops in *TI*, Vol. 10, London, 1973, pp. 50-70; ET of: *ST*, Bd. VIII, Einsiedeln, 1967, pp. 374-394.

Rahner, K., *The Priesthood*, New York, 1973; ET of: K. Rahner, *Einübung priesterlicher Existenz*, Freiburg, 1970; originally a series of retreat conferences given in 1961.

Rahner, K., *Priestly Existence* in *TI*, Vol. 3, London, 1967, pp. 239-262; ET of: *ST*, Bd. III, Einsiedeln, 1959 (Third Edition), pp. 285-312; first published in *ZAM* 17 (1942) 155-171.

Rahner, K., *Priestly Image*

Theological Reflections on the Priestly Image of Today and Tomorrow in *TI*, Vol. 12, London, 1974, pp. 39-60; ET of: *ST*, Bd. IX, Einsiedeln, 1970, pp. 373-394; first given in Munich at a conference, 28-29 June 1968.

Rahner, K., *Religious*
Religious Feeling Inside and Outside the Church in *TI*, Vol. 17, London, 1981, pp. 228-242; ET of: *ST*, Bd. XII, Einsiedeln, 1975, pp. 582-598; first published in *StdZ* 191 (1973) 3-13.

Rahner, K., *Shape*
The Shape of the Church to Come, London, 1974; ET of: *Strukturwandel der Kirche als Aufgabe und Chance*, Freiburg, 1972.

Rahner, K., *SL*
Servants of the Lord, London, 1968; pp. 47-216 of *SL* is the ET of: Rahner, K., *Knechte Christi. Meditationen zum Priestertum*, Freiburg, 1967.

Rahner, K., *Structure*
On the Structure of the People of the Church Today in *TI*, Vol. 12, London, 1974, pp. 218-228; ET of: *ST*, Bd. IX, Einsiedeln, 1970, pp. 558-568.

Rahner, K., *Teaching on Diaconate*
The Teaching of the Second Vatican Council on the Diaconate in *TI*, Vol. 10, London, 1973, pp. 222-232; ET of: *ST*, Bd. VIII, Einsiedeln, 1967, pp. 541-552; first published at a conference in Rome 22-24 October 1965.

Rahner, K., *Women*
Women and the Priesthood in *TI*, Vol. 20, London, 1981, pp. 35-47; ET of: *ST*, Bd. XIV, Einsiedeln, 1980, pp. 208-223 (the title in *ST* is: *Priestertum der Frau?*); first published in *StdZ* 195 (1977) 291-301.

2. Joint Works of Karl Rahner and Other Authors

Rahner, K., et al. (eds.), *SM*
Sacramentum Mundi. An Encyclopedia of Theology, 6 Volumes, New York, 1968-1970; ET of: Rahner, K., et al. (eds.), *Sacramentum Mundi. Theologisches Lexikon für Die Praxis*, IV Bände, Freiburg, 1967-1969.

Rahner, K., Ratzinger, J., *Episcopate*
The Episcopate and the Primacy (*QD*, 4), Freiburg, 1962; ET of: Rahner, K., Ratzinger, J., *Episcopat und Primat* (*QD*, 11), Freiburg, 1961 (= *EuP*).

3. Works of Other Authors

Bleistein, R., Klinger, E., *Bibliographie 1924-1969*
Bibliographie Karl Rahner 1924-1969, Freiburg, 1969.
Bühlmann, W., *The Church of the Future*, New York, 1986; ET of: *Welt Kirche: Neue Dimensionen — Modell für das Jahr 2001*, Graz, 1984.

Fahey, M., *Decade*
The Decade After the Council in O'Donovan, L. (ed.), *A Changing Ecclesiology* in *TS* 38 (1977) 754-762, esp. 755.
Hart, K., *The Juridical Status of Catechumens*, Rome, 1985.
van der Meer, H., *Women Priests in the Catholic Church? A Theological-Historical Investigation*, Philadelphia, 1973; ET of: *Priestertum der Frau? Eine theologische Untersuchung (QD,* 42), Freiburg, 1969.
O'Donovan, L. (ed.), *A Changing Ecclesiology*
A Changing Ecclesiology in a Changing Church: A Symposium on Development in the Ecclesiology of Karl Rahner in *TS* 38 (1977) 736-762.
O'Donovan, L., *Journey*
A Journey into Time: The Legacy of Karl Rahner's Last Years in *TS* 46 (1985) 621-646.
Schineller, P., *Early Foundations*
The Early Foundations in O'Donovan, L. (ed.), *A Changing Ecclesiology* in *TS* 38 (1977) 738-745.
Vorgrimler, H., *Understanding Karl Rahner*
Understanding Karl Rahner, An Introduction to His Life and Thought, London, 1986; ET of: *Karl Rahner verstehen. Eine Einführung in sein Leben und Denken,* Freiburg, 1985.
Vorgrimler, H. (ed.), *Wagnis*
Wagnis Theologie. Erfahrungen mit der Theologie Karl Rahners, Freiburg, 1979.
Wong, J., *Logos-Symbol*
Logos-Symbol in the Christology of Karl Rahner, Rome, 1984.

ABBREVIATIONS

1. Works of Karl Rahner

DK	Das Dynamische in der Kirche (= Dynamic Element in ET).
EP	The Episcopate and the Primacy, with Ratzinger, J.
FCF	Foundations of Christian Faith.
KC	Knechte Christi (= SL in ET).
SL	Servants of the Lord.
SM	Sacramentum Mundi, with others.
ST	Schriften zur Theologie, Bände I-XVI, Einsiedeln, 1954-1984.
TI	Theological Investigations, Volumes 1-22, London / New York, 1961-1990.

2. Other Abbreviations

AG   Ad gentes, Vatican II Decree on the Church's Missionary Activity.

Cath   Catholica, Münster, 1932-1939, 1952/53 ff.

ET   English translation.

GuL   Geist und Leben, Würzburg, 1947 ff.

LG   Lumen gentium, Vatican II Dogmatic Constitution on the Church.

StdZ   Stimmen der Zeit, Freiburg, 1915-1941, 1946/47 ff.

ZAM   Zeitschrift für Aszese und Mystik, Innsbruck, 1925-1944, since 1947 GuL.

ZKTh   Zeitschrift für katholische Theologie, Vienna, 1876/77-1943, 1947 ff.

RAHNER'S ECCLESIOLOGY

PART ONE

RAHNER'S ECCLESIOLOGY

Karl Rahner's writings on the church are significant both in regard to their number as well as their wide range of concern. There are three periods that help to highlight the development of his thinking about church: 1) his early writings, particularly looking at the years between the Second World War and the beginning of Vatican II; 2) his writings from approximately 1960-1965, the period from the immediate preparation of the Council until its conclusion; and 3) his writings following Vatican II up to his death in 1984.[1]

There is a two-fold advantage in following such a chronological approach to Rahner's ecclesiological writings: 1) Rahner has characterized his theological writings as originating in response to current specific questions or concerns; 2) a chronological approach enables us to focus upon the development of a person's position that occurs over an extended period of time. Thus, a particular ecclesiological theme treated by Rahner is less likely to be relativized in a chronological approach and can stand more on its own. In addition, it has been noted that Rahner's earlier work is at times more detailed and systematic than some aspects of his later work. This points to the fact that he frequently relies upon the conclusions of his earlier work as necessary stepping-off points for his later reflections.[2]

---

[1] This is the division presented by L. O'Donovan, in L. O'Donovan (ed.), *A Changing Ecclesiology in a Changing church: A Symposium on Development in the Ecclesiology of Karl Rahner* (hereafter *A Changing Ecclesiology*) in *TS* 38 (1977) 736-762, esp. 737. The third period posited by O'Donovan spans the "decade" following Vatican II. I would extend this third period to the death of Rahner in 1984.

[2] This is the interpretation of M. Fahey, *The Decade After The Council* (hereafter *Decade*) in L. O'Donovan (ed.), *A Changing Ecclesiology*, in *TS* 38

Is it possible to characterize Rahner's ecclesiology in one
particular way? Is there one complete systematization of his
ecclesiology? At first appearance, it might seem that the ecclesiological section of *Foundations of Christian Faith* would provide
this.[3] But one must recall Rahner's own introduction to the
book, in which he declares that this work should not be taken as
a "final summary" of his previous theological work.[4] This is
particularly evident in regard to his treatment of ecclesiology in
FCF. In a lecture in Freiburg in 1979, (three years after the
publication of *FCF*), he underscores the observation made by
Herbert Vorgrimler that he himself had omitted in this sixth
chapter "any reference to a theme on which I have elsewhere
written comparatively freshly and insistently — the theme of the
church of sinners, of the sinful church ... The ecclesiology of this
book has turned out to be perhaps too innocuous, even somewhat triumphalist."[5] This does not mean that one is justified in
disregarding the ecclesiological chapter in *FCF*. Rather, this
particular work itself must be critiqued and evaluated by recognizing the expressly stated purpose of the book, and by situating it
within Rahner's other ecclesiological writings.

It would be wrong, however, to consider Rahner's ecclesiology
as merely preliminary to a study of his sacramental theology of
ministerial office. The study of his ecclesiology is integral to an

(1977) 754-762, esp. 762: "Rahner's ecclesiology in the late 60's and 70's is
descriptive and phenomenological. Again it is characterized by probing analyses of
solutions and crises. In one sense it is less interdogmatic or systematic than it was
at an earlier stage, where Rahner was anxious to show more explicitly the
innerconnectedness of church and grace, church and Trinity, or church and
sacraments. He clearly presupposes that his present readers will have harked back
to his earlier basic writings."

    [3] Rahner, *Foundations of Christian Faith*, London, 1978, Chapter VII: *Chris-
tianity as Church*, pp. 322-401. This is the second largest section of *FCF*, preceded
in length only by Chapter VI: *Jesus Christ*, pp. 176-321.

    [4] Rahner, *FCF*, p. xv. Rahner describes the focus of *FCF* as the "first level of
reflection." His aim is to give an "intellectually honest justification of Christian
faith" (p. xii).

    [5] Rahner, *Foundations of Christian Faith* in *TI*, Vol. 19, London, 1984, pp. 3-
15, p. 14.

examination of the theme of ministerial office. The two are closely linked and intertwined with each other. In fact, one must consider the study of Rahner's ecclesiology as essentially belonging to a study of his sacramental theology of ministerial office. This is particularly evident in view of Rahner's affirmation of the church as *Grundsakrament* (fundamental sacrament) and his use of the terminology *Ursakrament* (primordial sacrament) to speak of Jesus Christ. A study of Rahner's ecclesiology is already a study of his sacramental theology of ministerial office.

EARLY ECCLESIOLOGICAL REFLECTIONS

There is no one systematic, comprehensive treatise on ecclesiology that Rahner has composed. Nevertheless, in his writings he deals with specific topics of ecclesiology as a systematic theologian. He relates themes in ecclesiology to his theology of grace, his christology, his pneumatology, and his sacramental theology. One cannot study Rahner's ecclesiology adequately outside of this context.[1] An attempt to study Rahner's ecclesiology in a fashion isolated from other areas of his theology would certainly result in an incomplete and possibly inaccurate picture.

1. E Latere Christi

Rahner's doctoral dissertation in theology, *E Latere Christi*,[2] presented and defended in 1936, reflects his interest in christology, exegesis, theology of symbol-sacramentology, and ecclesiology. Though this work was never published, it serves to indicate the inter-relatedness for Rahner of these various aspects of theology. "Rahner's *E Latere Christi* deals with ecclesiology as well as Christology and is hinged on the notion of the symbolic sign. ... The main typology applied to Christ in the dissertation is that of the new Adam from whose side the church as the new Eve is born. Analagous to the first Adam, Rahner states that the new Adam is the head of the new humanity, the origin of life."[3] Thus,

---

[1] P. Schineller, *The Early Foundations* (hereafter *Early Foundations*) in L. O'Donovan (ed.), *A Changing Ecclesiology* in *TS* 38 (1977) 738-745, esp. 738.

[2] For full reference, see, Bibliography.

[3] J. Wong, *Logos-Symbol in the Christology of Karl Rahner*, Rome, 1984, p. 44. All references to Rahner's unpublished theology doctoral dissertation is by means of citations in Wong's *Logos-Symbol*. Wong here cites *E Latere Christi*, p. 10.

even before Rahner began his theological teaching career, he had already focused on some aspects of the relationships between christology and ecclesiology.

2. The Individual in the church

It was ten years later, in 1946, that Rahner's "first important article in ecclesiology" was written.[4] The article was entitled, *The Individual in the Church*.[5] In it, Rahner deals with particular themes that continue to be a concern for him in later writings.

By his own admission, the principal motive for his reflection on the individual and the church is to encourage and challenge the individual Christian to a deeper living out of one's faith. There are three fundamental conclusions that Rahner reaches in the article in regard to this basic purpose. His first conclusion is that "because the individual is a unique spirit-person in religious matters too s/he has the right and the duty to make choices which

---

Wong further states that the dissertation "is an essay on the relation between Scripture and tradition, arguing that a certain patristic tradition was already implicitly present in Scripture itself. Rahner defends the thesis that the patristic tradition presenting Christ with blood and water flowing from his pierced side, as symbol of the new Adam, from whom the church as the new Eve was born, can be traced back to the Apostolic tradition" (pp. 40-41). In a note, Wong indicates that "Rahner attempted to establish this thesis through the combination of several NT texts, namely: Jn 19,34; Rom 5,12; and Eph 5, 25-27" (p. 41, n. 9).

[4] This is the judgment of P. Schineller, *Early Foundations*, p. 738. He also indicates two other early articles by Rahner dealing with ecclesiology: Rahner, *The Meaning of Frequent Confession of Devotion* in *TI*, Vol. 3, London, 1967; pp. 177-189, esp. pp. 184-186 (original, 1934) Rahner, *Priestly Existence* in *TI*, Vol. 3, London, 1967 (original, 1942), pp. 239-262, esp. pp. 247-249. P. Schineller indicates that in the 1934 article Rahner "speaks of God's presence in the world in a narrow and exclusivist sense as a presence occurring only through the church," whereas in the 1942 article "Rahner first makes the distinction between church in a broad sense, involving all those affected by the grace of Christ, and church in a narrower sense, referring to the visible church." G.P. Schineller, *Early Foundations*, p. 739, n. 4.

[5] Rahner, *The Individual in the Church* (hereafter *The Individual*) in Rahner, *Nature and Grace and other essays*, London, 1963, pp. 51-83.

cannot be directly governed by the church's law."[6] His second fundamental conclusion is that the action of a particular individual who carries out God's will in her/his life is truly carrying out charismatic action.[7] His third fundamental conclusion is that there is and should be a sphere of mutual solidarity of Christians among one another which as such is still not a participation or a sharing in the social organization of the church.[8]

a. The Individual's Right and Duty to Make Choices

The first of these conclusions deals with the right and the duty of the individual to make choices, and the fact that this process is not something in which the church directly participates. However, the key point being made by Rahner is not simply a negative statement about the church, but an emphasis that there is an imperative for the individual believer: to ask the question, "Lord, what do you want me to do?"[9] The danger, as Rahner sees it, is for the individual to hide behind the church. This collectivism within the church, notes Rahner, is rooted in "our own weariness and idleness which gladly forgoes the responsibility of making decisions." And it is quite clear that the danger described by Rahner as ecclesiastical collectivism is brought about "not by the church overstepping her limits, but by the individual not being able to hold out and bear responsibility any longer, and clinging onto the church's apron-strings, not by the church wanting to reduce her members to servitude, but by the masters themselves wanting to be enslaved."[10] Thus Rahner is not so much judging

---

[6] Rahner, *The Individual*, pp. 71-72. "Unique spirit-person" = eine geistig-personale Einmaligkeit, StdZ 139, p. 270.

[7] Rahner, *The Individual*, pp. 78-80.

[8] Rahner, *The Individual*, p. 80.

[9] Rahner, *The Individual*, pp. 72-73. See, also, P. Schillener, *Early Foundations*, p. 739: "Arguing almost exclusively from the viewpoint of philosophical and theological anthropology rather than from scripture or tradition, Rahner shows that although the church is truly a visible society with hierarchical authority, it may never forget that it is a society of free, individual persons."

[10] Rahner, *The Individual*, p. 75. The terminology of the original in the latter part of the quotation has particular importance in regard to interpreting termino-

the church structure to be flawed, but rather that individuals may not be accepting their responsibilities.

Fundamental to this first conclusion is Rahner's understanding of individuality. He notes that the concept of individuality is difficult to define. It is not so much the opposite to commonality "but rather correlative to it, and increases and decreases with it." Rahner explicitly states that "all the mistakes in this field arise from the failure to realize the analogical and correlative character of these concepts."[11] So, for example, individualism results if spirit-person individuality is raised to an absolute ideal which then determines what in regard to community may still remain on the level of sociality. (Sociality is the correlative concept with individuality on the level of materiality).[12] On the other hand, collectivism results if material-biological individuality is raised to an absolute ideal, and is normative in determining spirit-person individuality.

Therefore, for Rahner, as he himself notes, the term individuality "does not always mean the same thing." Its meaning can only be ascertained by locating the term on a continuum. At one extreme is the "individuated single being" which is completely closed in upon itself. At the other extreme is the "greatest mystery of our faith." The human being, says Rahner, is located between these two extremes: on the one hand, there is the "'death' of lifeless matter," and, on the other hand, the "infinite life of the Blessed Trinity."

For the human being, individuality is one reality which is composed of three levels. And each of these three levels must be seen in union with the other two levels. Thus, the human is: 1) a material individual; 2) a spiritual personality; and 3) a child of God. Subsequently, the way in which the One human being belongs to, (or, in a sense, relates to) the Many, corresponds to

---

logy used by Rahner to speak of bearers of ministerial office (i.e., *knechte Christi*), StdZ 139, p. 272.

[11] Rahner, *The Individual*, p. 55.

[12] Rahner, *The Individual*, p. 55; StdZ 139, p. 262. "Community" = *Gemeinschaft*; "Sociality" = *Gesellschaftlichen*.

these three levels of individuality: 1) society is the correlative term which corresponds to material-biological individuality; 2) community is the correlative term which corresponds to spirit-person individuality; and 3) union in Christ is the correlative term which corresponds to what Rahner speaks of as theological individuality.

Based on the mutual interpenetration of the three levels of individuality that cannot be isolated from each other, Rahner reaches some important conclusions. Society, for example, is not a herd, since society can be realized as a genuine human reality through the spirit-person individuality of human beings. But although Rahner does not mention this explicitly, society would be seen as "herd" insofar as spirit-person individuality fails to realize more than the material-biological level of human existence. As is so often the case, Rahner focuses on the aspect of possibility, namely, that society is able to be realized as human society. But the very possibility must admit that the spirit-person individuality can also freely choose not to "humanize" society, even though society "requires" that it be affirmed as more than a material-biological reality. Therefore, were the individual to do nothing in this regard, the consequent result would be a reality that would exhibit more of the qualities of a herd.

A second example that Rahner presents as a conclusion is that spirit-person individuality is not an "angel-like heavenly hierarchy", since spirit-person individuality requires the mediation that can only be given by material-biological individuality. Thus, material-biological individuality necessarily constitutes the possibility for spirit-person individuality. Rahner clearly emphasizes the mutuality with regard to material-biological individuality and spirit-person individuality, rejecting a view which would "spiritualize" the individual. The individual human being's transcendentality is necessarily realized in history.

The picture that emerges, therefore, says Rahner, is that the One individuality and the belonging to the Many are "not conflicting but complementary concepts," both in regard to human individuality itself and specifically in regard to the human being who necessarily partakes in the reality of the Many.[13] Following from this, Rahner holds that the real problematic consists in the proper balance and in the reciprocal consideration between the individuality on one level and the plurality on the other level of the make-up of human, layered existence.[14] Rahner indicates that a specific example of this problematic is seen in the case of the relationship between the church as society and the individual as a spirit-person-graced individual.

Theological individuality expresses for Rahner the reality of the human being as a graced individual. The correlative term "union in Christ" describes this aspect of the One individual in relationship to the Many. Grace is always the self-communication of God to the individual in a unique and absolutely singular way. "God gives Oneself to each directly without anything whatever coming between. And this in spite of, or rather because of, the mediation of all grace through Christ the mediator and his church, whose purpose is not to come between God and the human being in the manner of neo-platonic Areopagitical cosmic hierarchy of mediations, but to give each human being immediate access to God."[15] The self-communication of God is always the self-communication of the one God, and so the fundamental unity of God with all

---

[13] Rahner, *The Individual*, pp. 59-60. "Many" = *Vielheit*. The ET incorrectly translates *Vielheit* as "community."

[14] Rahner, *The Individual*, p. 60. The ET is incomplete and confusing. The original: "Die echte Problematik liegt vielmehr im rechtigen Ausgleich und in der gegenseitigen Rücksichtnahme zwischen der Einzelheit einer Stufe und der Vielheit einer anderen Stufe des menschlichen geschichteten Wesensgefüges," StdZ 139, p. 264, is translated: "The really difficult problem is to find the right balance and the true recognition of each other between individuality on the one level and community on the other levels."

[15] Rahner, *The Individual*, p. 60. The ET of this very fundamental statement by Rahner regarding theological individuality is basically faithful to the original, but the language of the original is much more precise: "(Gott) der sich jedem Menschen in absoluter Unmittelbarkeit in der Gnade mitteilt trotz, nein wegen der Vermitteltheit aller Gnade durch den Mittler Christus und seine Kirche, deren Sinn es gerade ist, den unmittelbaren Zugang jedes Einzelnen zu Gott selbst zu begründen, nicht aber als 'Mittleres' im Sinne einen neuplatonischen oder areopagitischen Stufenbaus des Kosmos zwischen Gott und der Seele zu stehen," StdZ 139, p. 265.

individuals is both the beginning and end point of God's self-communication. But God's offer of self-communication is an offer to the individual both as spirit-person individual —in uniqueness— as well as material-biological individual —in solidarity with others. The great "discovery" of Christianity is to disclose the unique irreplaceability of the individual "who makes her/himself what s/he will be for eternity." But the working out itself of what the individual becomes necessarily takes place in solidarity with others.

A further aspect of the spirit-person-graced individual is highlighted through an appreciation of the ethical and moral-theological perspective. It is precisely only through the exercise of her/his free choice that the individual determines her/his own unique definitiveness. Therefore, the individual is morally bound to exercise this free choice. This morally binding responsibility is rooted in the uniqueness of the individual. Consequently, "there is an individual morality which is binding on the individual as uniquely for her/him, and this cannot be called a mere application of a universal principle to one case."[16] Accordingly, the individual is called to exercise free choice not in an arbitrary way, but rather to recognize what is God's morally binding will for her or him as an individual. And it is specifically through the exercise of conscience that the individual can achieve this. Yet, conscience itself can be seen to have two similar but distinct functions: 1) "the one which tells a human being's subjective self the universal norms of ethics and moral theology and then applies them to her/his 'case'; and 2) the one by which the individual hears God's call to her/him alone which can never be fully deduced from universal norms."[17] This latter function of conscience can be realized only in practice; it is an important skill in the fullest sense of the word.

---

[16] Rahner, *The Individual*, pp. 61-62. "There is a sphere of individual morality and religion [that], ... while it never conflicts with the universal moral law, nevertheless has the decisive word over and above it and can no longer be contained in it. Of course there is not, and must not be, an individual morality which sets itself up against the universal moral law ..." (p. 62).

[17] Rahner, *The Individual*, pp. 62-63.

And Rahner goes on to state that "if we were to look for a traditional name for it we would call it the charismatic act of 'discernment of spirits.'" And what is this discernment of spirits? It is "the ability to hear and recognize God's call to this human being alone among the many voices all calling her/him in different directions, the 'spirits.'"[18]

It is this art of discernment of spirits that achieves in a practical way this first of Rahner's fundamental conclusions regarding the individual and the church. To repeat that conclusion is to see how closely it is linked with Rahner's insistence that the discernment of spirits be so central for the individual in the church: "because the individual is a unique spirit-person in religious matters too s/he has the right and the duty to make choices which cannot be directly governed by the church's law."[19]

b. The Individual's Charismatic Action

The second conclusion that Rahner arrives at regarding the individual in the church is that the individual who carries out God's will in her/his life is truly carrying out charismatic action. Rahner distinguishes that such an action of an individual is not merely the result of a regular personal decision in which the unique will of God is discerned, but is specifically itself a graced, God-gifted action. That is, it is not only an action achieved by means of grace, but specifically charismatic action.

For Rahner, the notion of charism is rooted in the unmediated encounter between God and the individual. He refers to Paul in affirming that each individual has her/his charism, gift, vocation. And he states that it is wrong to conceive of charism as something that is primarily extraordinary or miraculous. At heart, to affirm the reality of charism is to affirm that the Holy Spirit is at work in the church in an unmediated way. This means that the

---

[18] Rahner, *The Individual*, pp. 63-64.
[19] Rahner, *The Individual*, pp. 71-72.

law of the church is not able to predetermine with certainty the direction in which the Spirit moves in particular, unfolding historical events. The charismatic element, which Rahner describes as "dynamic unrest if not (specifically) revolutionary upheaval," is an established essential element of the church.

The charismatic element in the church is centered on the individual, because it is here that the unmediated encounter with God takes place. "The charismatic element in the church is what is unique by grace in the church, the individual's right by grace in the church and for the church."[20] Therefore, Rahner affirms that grace and the impetus to act does not take place only through the church's "institutional sacraments, commandments and official guidance and ruling." A difficulty, however, is that "in practice we cannot clearly distinguish it (the charismatic element of the individual) from the level of spiritual-personal individuality, which in itself still belongs to the natural sphere, even though it works itself out in the religious sphere too."[21]

Nevertheless, though recognizing this difficulty, Rahner insists that all who hold office in the church, indeed, all who make up the church, have a responsibility to acknowledge and value the charismatic element in the church. The point, says Rahner, is that the Spirit of God does not necessarily fall upon the officially appointed shepherds of the church. Rather, children, virgins, and the poor in spirit can also be people of vision, people who are truly prophets, people who "can learn from God a new way of being a Christian and a new Christian way of life, and can receive from God a mission to show this to the church of their time."[22]

Rahner's second conclusion regarding the individual in the church, that of the charismatic element, is further highlighted by studying the reality of church itself.

Rahner defines church in a two-fold way. It is: "the community of the redeemed bound together 'intrinsically' in Christ Jesus, and

[20] Rahner, *The Individual*, p. 78.

[21] Rahner, *The Individual*, p. 78. Rahner focuses specifically on the relationship between nature and grace.

[22] Rahner, *The Individual*, p. 79.

at the same time a visible organized society with rules and
founder's charter. Neither truth about the church should be
separated from or confused with the other."[23] The two dangers
that Rahner notes are: 1) to see the church only as the solidarity
of the redeemed that is brought about by grace; a solidarity
which, by definition, is beyond or transcends the empirical; and
2) to see the church only as a juridically organized society, as a
"Salvation-Institution."

The relationship between these two elements of church is a
particularly nuanced one. For in spite of the fact that they both
belong to the full realization of one church, and in spite of the
fact that in some way the one element, the "institutional," is the
sacramental, brought-about-by-sign visibility of the other, nevertheless, Rahner affirms that the two do not adequately coincide,
the one with the other. He insists that these not be seen as two
aspects of one and the same reality, so that the two would
necessarily always occur or appear together.[24] He gives two cases
to illustrate his point. It is possible that an individual can belong
to the community —brought about by grace— of those who are
redeemed in Christ, without this individual being a member of the
visible, juridically organized church as such. And a second
example, one which Rahner notes is indisputable church dogma,
is the case of an individual who is clearly a member of the visible,
juridically organized church, but is separated from the graced-
community of all in Christ because of sin-unto-death.

The conclusions that Rahner reaches are that the grace-
community and the juridical-society are mutually ordered, and
together belong to a full understanding of church. But, nevertheless, these are two different elements, which lie in entirely different
sociological spheres, and have come to be in different ways.
Consequently, it follows that it is an entirely different matter to
determine the relationship of the individual to the community of

[23] Rahner, *The Individual*, p. 64.
[24] Rahner, *The Individual*, pp. 64-65. (ET is misleading; Rahner's emphasis is
on the fact that these two elements do not necessarily coincide.)

the church and to determine the relationship of the individual to the society of the church.

The church as a grace-community is correlative to spirit-person-graced individuality. The church as a juridically structured society is correlative to material-biological individuality. And it is ultimately through the fact of the material-biological layer of one's existence that the individual is affirmed as a univocal member of a multitude of identical individuals. Such an individual is one who is a moral and ontological individual who can and must be subject to practical laws, to regulations from an external authority, to compulsion, and so forth. And so Rahner repeats his earlier-stated conviction that the real difficulty lies only in the relationship between the spirit-person individual and the church as juridically organized society. Rahner consequently focuses upon this relationship and offers the following reflections.

There is for each human being, specifically as spirit-person individual, what Rahner calls a private sphere, which the church, as juridically organized society, is not permitted or allowed to touch directly. Yet, Rahner states that this private sphere cannot be seen to be private in an absolute sense. For, based on the unity of the human being, and the given interpenetration of the individual's metaphysical layers, specifically spirit-person individuality, the church indirectly encounters even this private sphere. But, nevertheless, Rahner asserts that there is this private sphere in principle which is not directly accessible by the church as juridically organized society.

It is proper, Rahner says, to distinguish between those things which are beneath a society's authority, which in themselves are essentially unimportant, from those things which Rahner describes as being above society's authority. It is the latter which, Rahner says, reach immediately to the individual's private sphere. Thus, even though Rahner emphasizes that the private sphere is fundamentally a conceptual distinction, and not a real distinction discernible within the individual, he nevertheless affirms this private sphere as necessary for the individual. And therefore he concludes that "there can and should be actions which are the

expression of a human being's personal and Christian uniqueness," even though they are in themselves specifically not accessible to any ecclesiastical authority.[25]

Rahner offers additional support for this principle by noting that
the church actually acknowledges and holds it in high regard.
Specifically, the church has not claimed the right to definitively
judge the ultimate moral state of an individual human being
standing before God. And the reason is not due to the practical
difficulties that this would involve, but because there is no "ecclesial human judgment day" by which a human being can be judged
in an ultimate way. Additionally, Rahner notes the fact that the
church, as juridically organized society, renounces the right to
bring about by force the baptism and the acceptance of the faith
by those who are unbaptized. And so, one is led to ask what
fundamental insights in this regard must necessarily be carried over
in the church's (as juridically organized society) relations with the
baptized. But the most evident point, according to Rahner, is that
there exists a "private religious life" that is quite distinct from the
"official juridical life" of the church. A large number of things are
entrusted to the personal judgment of the individual, such as: what
an individual Christian thinks, and reads, and prays, and what
religious vocation an individual may follow. If there were no
"private religious life," the consequence would be that the church
as juridically organized society would be required, in Rahner's
words, "to set up an obligatory ecclesiastical appointments office
to decide everyone's vocation in the church under pain of sin,
decide who are to be priests, which women are to be parish
helpers, who are to be on the parish council." To deny the reality
of this private religious sphere would necessarily mean that the
church as juridically organized society would carry on a "religious
dictatorship" and a "collectivism".

---

[25] Rahner, *The Individual*, pp. 68-69. The present text is based upon the
original. The ET is wrong due to the failure to translate the negative term: *keiner*.
Original: "Es kann und soll daher Handlungen geben, die zum Ausdruck der
personalen christlichen Einmaligkeit werden sollen, obwohl sie an sich auch keiner
kirchlichen Regelung zugänglich sind."

c. Individuals and "Private Religious Community Life"

Rahner's third basic conclusion, as first indicated above, is closely related to and follows from his considerations on the "private religious sphere" of the individual. Rahner points to the social connections within this sphere, stating that that which is private on the part of the individual can and should have an influence upon other human beings. Therefore, Rahner concludes that there is and should be a sphere of mutual solidarity of Christians among one another which as such is still not a participation or sharing in the social organization of the church.

There are a number of activities, according to Rahner, which exemplify this as a reality already existing. When two Christians pray with one another, when one Christian offers a spiritually enlightening word to another, or when one Christian comforts another in the power of the Holy Spirit, there life is at work which is truly Christian and at the same time truly private. It is a reality which a juridical organization of a church variety would not be able to replace or to repress, as necessary and useful as such organizations are. This reality Rahner describes as being something like a movement; he suggests the name "free groups".

These free groups, which have a fundamental concern for the other, have their origin from individuals, and do not derive their life from the official organization. They are made up of individuals whom Rahner describes as "charismatics without office in the church."[26] And while such individuals do not have the benefit of the church's mission to influence other church members, nevertheless, Rahner insists that obstacles motivated by "unenlightened zeal, or jealousy or a bureaucratic mania" should not be put in the way by the church as juridically organized society. Such obstacles evince what Rahner describes as church totalitarianism.

In the end, the most important emphasis, as Rahner sees it, is to reaffirm the important place that "private religious community

[26] Rahner, *The Individual*, p. 81.

life" must have. Perhaps unconsciously adapting the terminology of Mark 2:27, Rahner stresses that the church, as juridically organized society, is for the human being, and not the human being for the church, and that all official church organization forms and structures —if they themselves are necessary and of divine law— still have a subsidiary character to the private religious community life which they should not absorb, but should foster, protect, and complete.

Rahner uses an additional phrase to speak of individuals who are truly living a private religious life for others: "lay charismatics." But he points out that both the terminology as well as the reality are not established in opposition to the "ideal of the Latin church to get charismatics with office or charismatic officials, or to put it more simply, holy priests." [27] On the contrary, he says that "when a new pentecostal wind blows directly on the official church, this is the best possible balance between office (*Amt*) and spiritual gift (*Pneuma*), between the charismatic individual and the social organization of the church." [28]

Conclusion

It is noteworthy that Rahner's words about a new pentecostal wind blowing directly on the official church were composed in 1946. It would be thirteen years before John XXIII would initiate the steps leading to Vatican II. Certainly Rahner's ecclesiological reflections at this early date did not stand alone. But his insights and the concerns that he manifested regarding the individual in the church would continue to occupy his writings.

His final thoughts at this early stage view the relationship of the individual and the church as an extremely rich and nuanced relationship. He sees the eschatological fulfillment of the kingdom as realizing the deepest encounter of each individual with God.

---

[27] Rahner, *The Individual*, p. 82.
[28] Rahner, *The Individual*, p. 82.

But, he says, now there is still the church, the visible church. And the church renders the individual free and gains for the individual her or his own individuality, in that the individual, in humble and faithful love, is always giving her/himself selflessly within the church.

3. Membership of the church

A year after Rahner's article on the individual in the church, he published a second important ecclesiological essay dealing with membership in the church.[29] As indicated in the lengthy title, the publication of Pius XII's encyclical *Mystici Corporis Christi* on 29 June 1943 was the context and particular motivation for Rahner to present these ecclesiological reflections. Specifically, Rahner sought to respond to three questions pertinent to the encyclical: 1) "Who, according to the teaching laid down in this encyclical, belong to the church as members in the fullest sense and who do not belong in this sense?" 2) "What follows, or what does not necessarily follow with regard to justification, state of grace, and union with Christ for this kind of non-membership of the church?" and 3) "What insights into the nature of the church itself result from this teaching about membership and non-membership of the church?"

Rahner himself notes the criticism that he had chosen an extremely narrow approach in focusing so exclusively on the recent encyclical. But he defends his starting-point as one which provides an opportunity for fundamental ecclesiological considerations. It also exemplifies a recurrent interest on Rahner's part to relate his theological reflections explicitly to church tradition. In this context, it means situating the encyclical in the broad expanse of church tradition on the question of church membership. Only from such a context can an accurate interpretation of the encyclical take place.

[29] Rahner, *Membership of the Church According to the Teaching of Pius XII's Encyclical 'Mystici Corporis Christi'* (hereafter *Membership*) in *TI*, 2, London, 1963, pp. 1-88.

But an equally important motive for Rahner focusing on the encyclical is his ecumenical concern. He states that it would be "very sad and most regrettable" if as a result of the encyclical there occurred a widening of the gulf between Catholics and non-Catholics. Can the encylical, Rahner asks, actually contribute to the realization of church unity? It is his hope that it can.

A final response by Rahner to the criticism that his focus is too narrow is his firm conviction that the question of church membership necessarily raises the question of the nature of the church itself.

a. The Concept of the Church: Sacrament

Rahner proposes that the nature of the church can be clarified in a very significant way by an appreciation of the concept of sacrament. Consequently, in a certain way, it is very difficult, if not impossible, to separate Rahner's ecclesiology from his sacramentology.

Rahner views the reality of sacrament as exemplifying the "general structure of Christian reality." And this ultimately is rooted in the fact that Jesus Christ is fully human and fully divine. "Just as in Christ himself the divine nature and the human nature are as such unmixed and necessarily to be distinguished as they are unseparated, so it is also in the case of the sacraments and elsewhere in Christian reality."[30]

In terms of the church, Rahner states that this manifests itself in the very nature of the church. There is, as Rahner indicates, a double concept of church, which he chooses to describe here by applying the term *Ursakrament* to the church.[31] On the one hand, there is the concept of the church "as incarnate presence of Christ and his grace, together with Christ and his grace." And on

[30] Rahner, *Membership*, p. 73. He speaks of the *ungetrennte und unvermischte Gottmenschlichkeit der Kirche*.

[31] Rahner, *Membership*, p. 73. Rahner is very clear in stressing that he is speaking of two concepts of the church "and not of two churches" with the result that one "might then be asked how far they 'coincide' or do not coincide with one another" (p. 76; n. 91).

the other hand there is the concept of church "in as far as she must essentially be distinguished from this grace and inner divine union, without ceasing, however, to be even in this way a still valid Christian reality."[32] In both cases, these concepts of church parallel a double concept of sacrament, that is: 1) sacrament as "sign and grace", and 2) sacrament as "valid sacramental sign" insofar as a valid sacramental sign can be thought of and can exist without the working of grace.

What is essential in regard to Rahner's sacramentology and, hence, in this case, in regard to his ecclesiology, is that these two concepts are "necessary and indispensible, neither can replace the other; they must not be played off one against the other."[33] Therefore, it would be wrong to give preference to one concept of the church over the other. In fact, a particular danger would be to affirm only the concept of church as sign and grace, concluding that it is the full concept. To do this fails to recognize that the human being "does not and cannot, in the last resort, grasp or determine the interior event of grace." And so, one must equally affirm the concept of the church as a "visible, and sacramentally and juridically verifiable" Christian reality. And it is precisely this concept of the church that must be the first and most engaging for the human being. For Rahner notes in regard to sacrament that "one asks first of all about the sacramental happening as such, in as far as this must be essentially distinguished, although not really separated, from sacramental grace as such."[34]

As to the ultimate reason why Rahner emphasizes this double concept of church, he states that on the one hand it is necessary to safeguard the incarnational principle of Christianity, and on the other hand to affirm the grace of God as the mystery of the incomprehensible God.

The theological interpretation that Rahner offers for the church that is empty of grace is rooted in the event of the crucifixion. In the crucifixion the reality of God-emptiness becomes the actual

[32] Rahner, *Membership*, pp. 73-74.

[33] Rahner, *Membership*, p. 72.

[34] Rahner, *Membership*, p. 73.

manifestation of God in the world. Similarly, the church, which is the "real, permanent and ever valid presence of God in the world," continues to be this even when the church is a sinful church.

In a corollary fashion, Rahner views membership of the church in terms of sacramentology. This membership, he says, "in its external juridical verifiability," is the "basic sacramental sign" (*sakramentale Urzeichen*; more exactly: "sacramental primordial sign") of the gracing of the individual. And so, even when the individual member of the church, as a sinner, lessens or irrevocably loses the reality of grace, that membership still is valid. For such membership —paradoxically— declares and affirms God as the mystery that even one who is a member of the church must accept. Thus, accepting the mystery of the incomprehensible God requires necessarily renouncing any ultimate certainty with regard to God's free self-gift.[35]

b. The People of God

The church is the visibility of God's grace. This very visibility is identified by Rahner as a multi-leveled reality. One level of this visibleness of God's grace is termed by Rahner "people of God." The term evinces a reality which is radically Christological and anthropological. "This real determination of the one humanity as the people of God is a real fact and no mere abstract idea of what ought to be, for it is based on the two coinciding facts of (1) the natural unity of the human race and (2) of the real Incarnation of the Word of God."

Rahner emphasizes that this fundamental unity of humanity belongs to the reality of visibleness. For this visibleness itself is

---

[35] Rahner, *Membership*, p. 76. Significant in discussing the question of membership of the church in terms of sacramentology is the relationship between *potestas iurisdictionis* (power of jurisdiction) and *potestas ordinis* (power of order). Rahner notes that "these two powers are together the basis of the visible nature and visible unity of the church, since authority is the source of the unity, community (*Gesellschaft*; better translated: "society") and consequent visibleness of a *societas perfecta*."

rooted in the human being, affirmed as spirit and matter. From this follows the distinction betwen human being as intelligible person and as nature. Naturally, however, these two levels can never be separated from one another. But the significance in all this, says Rahner, is that it points out that the revelation of the human being's own uniqueness essentially always happens specifically in the acceptance of what is alien to the individual, that is, in the acceptance of the imposed certainty of one's nature.[36]

Also constituting this reality of the visibleness of human beings is the fact of the Incarnation. The Incarnation means that already in advance, really-ontologically, humanity has gone on to realize the actual grace-achieving holiness of the individual human being, has gone on to become the people of God. It is from the event of the Incarnation, that is, of God's becoming a human being, that Rahner looks to the time previous as well as to the time following. The theological context for Rahner of the Incarnation is the universal salvific will of God for all people. The Incarnation, as a given historical event, is the basic starting-point for this understanding.

What the Incarnation indicates is that "in as far as humanity, thus 'consecrated,' is a real unity from the very start, there already exists a 'people of God' which extends as far as humanity itself, even before any social and juridical organization of humanity as a supernatural unity in a church." What is important to note is that this realization of the oneness of humanity occurs in innumerable expressions of intensity. But, where it occurs, Rahner predicates of that event the term "people of God."

Ultimately, what Rahner wishes to stress is that there exists a curious relationship between the people of God and the church. There is similarity in that both are realities which touch the individual human being on the level of visibleness. And also that

---

[36] Rahner, *Membership*, p. 81. At heart here is the dialectic for the human being between "what is freely willed as such and what is freely done" (p. 80). for Rahner stresses that it is necessary that the expression and the revelation of an individual's free choice take place in the individual's visibleness, but this visibleness itself can "throw a veil over" the individual's free choice in the sense that what results can be "mere empty appearance".

both are the expression in the world of the loving, saving will of God. Both realities can also be seen in relation to the Incarnation. For the acceptance on the part of God of a human nature is as such again the mere expression and becoming-visible of God's will which intends the union of all persons with God in grace — now— and in glory —beyond death.[37] The church itself should be the expression and visibleness of the fact that in Christ humanity is the people of God.[38]

But Rahner underscores that the gradual realization of this complete and final union takes place in some measure outside of the socially and juridically organized church. He comes to the conclusion that "where there is, and to the extent in which there is the people of God, there already is radically also the church, and that independently of the will of the individual human being."[39] And the real effect of this event is that the church on the social and juridical level is concretized.

The relationship between membership in the people of God and membership in the church also highlights the curious relationship between these two realities. Any individual who freely chooses to carry out God's will in her/his life is enabled to do that because of the gift of God's very self. And the expression of this justifying act must of necessity take place in some manner of visibleness. And it is this visibleness that Rahner refers to as membership of the people of God. Rahner is not saying that each human being automatically through birth is a member of the people of God. It is the result, the expression of an individual's freely chosen justifying act. Rahner insists that one can only conclude thus, because the justifying act itself must find expres-

---

[37] Rahner, *Membership*, p. 83. "Curious" = *eigentümlich*. It is important to situate Rahner's statement that the Incarnation is the "mere" expression of God's will both in the full context of Rahner's Christology and specifically what he sees as the relationship between history and transcendence.

[38] Rahner, *Membership*, pp. 83-84. The ET of this passage poorly renders the original. Rahner is not positing people of God as an independent, objective reality completely different from the objective reality of church. Both rather evince the multi-leveled reality of the visibleness of that unity which is achieved by God.

[39] Rahner, *Membership*, p. 84.

sion in "something really different from itself, namely in membership of the people of God."[40] And this membership in the people of God "is in reality ordained to membership of the church in the proper sense."[41]

Rahner's reflections on the reality of the people of God indicate more clearly the importance of sacrament in his ecclesiology. He notes that the juridical and social organization and also the human being's union with God by grace belong to the full concept of church. Thus, it is in regard to the church in its juridical and social organization, ("as something visible and as a sign of the union with God by grace"), that he posits a "further twofold reality: (1) church as an established juridical organization in the sacred order,[42] and (2) church as humanity consecrated by the Incarnation."

Rahner's motivation for insisting on both of these realities is his concern that the human dimension of ecclesiology will diminish or be done away with. It is not possible, he states, for a justified person, who is not a member of the church, to belong to the visible church in a "merely invisible" way. Instead, "the justified person who belongs (or is 'referred') to the church without being a member of it, belongs 'invisibly' to the visible

[40] Rahner, *Membership*, p. 84.

[41] Rahner, *Membership*, p. 84. In regard to the question of membership of the church, Rahner finds completely unacceptable the distinction between "constitutional membership," achieved through baptism alone, and "operative membership," which is exemplified by the actual presence of grace. Such an approach fails to see that "it is quite clear and definite from the church's doctrinal pronoucements that the church is an undivided and visible quantity which essentially requires for its constitution the unity of Faith and Law," pp. 17-19, esp. p. 19. He will go on to propose that an acceptable and worthwhile distinction can be made between "belonging" and "being a member": "'being a member' (of the actual kind) is something which does not admit of degrees (one either is or is not a member) whereas 'belonging' does admit of degrees; the highest and fullest of which is precisely membership itself."

[42] Rahner, *Membership*, p. 86. In n. 97, Rahner adds that the church as a juridical organization has three dimensions which correspond to the three conditions for strict membership in the church: 1) unity of faith under the authoritative magisterium; 2) visibility of grace in virtue of the sacraments (above all in baptism and the Eucharist); and 3) united action under the direction of the ecclesiastical ruling authority.

church by grace and has a 'visible' relation to this church, even
when this relation is not constituted by baptism or by an exter-
nally verifiable profession of the true faith (as in the case of the
catechumen)."[43] Clearly, Rahner wants to avoid any form of
ecclesiology which could be described in parallel terms to Christological monophysitism. It is important to both recognize and
safeguard the inseparability of "the human being's state of grace
and its quasi-sacramental tangibility."

The acceptance of the grace of God requires that this acceptance attain to a certain visibleness. Grace, the self-gift of God to
human beings, necessarily takes place in the spatio-temporal
visibleness of humanity. On the other hand, it is important to
recognize that the reverse is possible. There can be the sign-reality
of grace without this grace being personally accepted. An adult
individual, for example, can be validly baptized, but it is possible
that this individual does not encounter the graced self-gift of
God's love. This possibility is ultimately one that is situated in
the context of the question of sin and the church. This is a topic
to which Rahner gives serious attention.

4. Church of Sinners — Sinful Church

As indicated above, Rahner recognizes that the ecclesiology
presented in *Foundations of Christian Faith* lacks an important
consideration, namely the relationship between the church and
sin. The earliest treatment of this specific theme belongs to the
early period of Rahner's ecclesiological writings. In an article
published in 1947 Rahner focuses on the reality of sin and the
church.[44] He gives a two-fold approach. On the one hand, he

---

[43] Rahner, *Membership*, p. 87. In regard to the relationship of the catechumen
to the juridically and socially organized church, see K. Hart, *The Juridical Status
of Catechumens*, Rome, 1985.

[44] Rahner, *The Church of Sinners* (hereafter *Church of Sinners*) in *TI*, Vol. 6,
London, 1969, pp. 253-269; ET of: *ST*, Bd. VI, Einsiedeln, 1965, pp. 301-320.
First published in StdZ 72 (1947) 163-177. (Also of note is that this article was the
second of Rahner's writings to be published in ET, appearing in *Cross Currents* 3

investigates what it means to speak of sinners in the church and the sinful church. And on the other hand, a more pastoral question is how individual members of the church cope with the fact of the church's sinfulness.

a. Sinners in the Church and the Sinful Church

Rahner first considers the reality of sin and the church from a dogmatic perspective, and only subsequently does he address the question from the —not unimportant— pastoral perspective. While human experience all too clearly recognizes the reality of sin and the church, the necessary starting-point for Rahner is God's revelation itself which discloses this reality. Both in the history of dogma and in the faith-history of individuals, the church has frequently been rejected precisely because it does not appear to correspond to one's professed belief in the "holy" church. The reality which Rahner sees is that the church truly has been bestowed with holiness, and so is a holy church. But there is also a holiness which the church does not possess.

Sinners belong to the church. Yet, says Rahner, this is not a self-evident truth. What is self-evident is that "respectable people," "virtuous people," people who are "saints" belong to a "socially recognized religious association known as the Catholic church. And so, to declare, with church tradition, that the sinner belongs to the church is to declare that an individual who is lacking the grace of God, who is walking far from God, is actually a member of the church, a part of the visibleness of God's grace in the world, a member of the Body of Christ. Yet it is necessary to recognize that "the sinner does not belong to the church in the same full sense as the justified person."

Rahner interprets this reality of the sinner belonging to the church by means of sacramentology. Referring to the church as

(1951) 64-74. The first of his works appearing in ET was the article *Multiplication of Masses*, published in *Orate Fratres* 24 (1950) 553-562, See, in this regard, R. Bleistein, E. Klinger, *Bibliographie 1924-1969*, pp. 19, entry n. 203, and p. 20, entry n. 227.)

Ursakrament, he distinguishes between the visible embodiment of the church insofar as the church is a sign of grace, and on the other hand insofar as the church is a reality filled with grace. The sinner continues to belong to the visible embodiment of the church, but this belonging is no longer the "efficacious sign of her/his invisible membership of the church as a living, holy community." In a certain sense, the sinner has made her/his belonging to the church into a lie.

What does it mean to declare that there are truly sinners "in" the church? This is a crucial question for Rahner. For if one were to admit that there are indeed sinners in the church, but that this has nothing to do with the real church, the result would be a highly suspect, idealistic concept of church. But if the church "is something real, and if her members are sinners and as sinners remain members, then she herself is sinful." The most remarkable point here, according to Rahner, is that this truth that the church itself is sinful is first and foremost a truth of faith, and not something merely arrived at by means of a sociological, empirical study.

Equally as much a truth of faith is the fact that the "official ministerial representatives" of the church "can be," "have been," and "are sinners" in a very noticeable way. Since the activity of the church is not something that occurs through an abstract principle nor through the Holy Spirit alone, but as an activity of human beings, Rahner holds that one must conclude that the church can be sinful in its actions. He strongly rejects a dualism which would not predicate the sinful acts of individual official representatives as truly being acts of the church. Such sinful activity takes place in opposition to the inner impulse of the Holy Spirit, but nevertheless it takes place. Yet, one is led to affirm in faith that this sinful church itself is the very bride of Christ, that it is the vessel of the Holy Spirit.[45]

---

[45] Rahner, *Church of Sinners*, p. 261. Rahner stresses that an individual is not justified in breaking away from the church because s/he has judged that the church has ceased to be the ideal church that it once was.

This church, which never ceases to be human, remains in life-filled solidarity with Christ, who is the source of all holiness. And this church, whose foundation of life is the Holy Spirit, moves toward the day when the Holy God will manifest himself in an unveiled way in his world. On that day, the church, which has the form of a sinner, will be revealed for what the church is in reality.

The unique character of the church's sin is that only this sin can distort and conceal the visibleness of Christ in the world, which is precisely what the church is. Yet, the unique quality of the church's holiness means that, unlike all other historical organizations, the church's sin can never so distort the visibleness of Christ in the world that the Holy Spirit would depart from the church or be unable any longer to manifest God historically and visibly. This is because the Holy Spirit has inseparably united itself to the church.[46]

Rahner is very hesitant to recommend vocal protests against scandals that occur in the church. He says that protest can often be called for, and may even be praiseworthy. However, his critique is that the motivation for such protest may be, not a willingness to directly face sin, but the expression of anger that one encounters in oneself because of the consequences of sin.

The sin of the church gives to the church the real possibility of bringing its suffering to an end, of overcoming its sin. But it must recognize its sin to do this. The theological foundation that allows the church to do this is the cross of Christ. When the church suffers by its sin, it incurs redemption from its guilt. For the church suffers this guilt in Christ, the crucified one. Sin manifests itself necessarily in the world, in the church, as the consequence of what takes place in the heart. Thus sin, in its historical and social reality can be overcome by Christ crucified,

---

[46] Rahner, *Church of Sinners*, p. 263. Sin for the human being, notes Rahner, lies essentially on a level "deeper" than the social and the historical. It has its existential origin in the heart. Sin itself always necessarily happens in a historical and social context. But when there is sin of the church, this sin does not reveal what the church is at the deepest level. Rather, this sin distorts, veils, and contradicts the reality of the church.

who is the historical and social realization of the gift of God's love.

None of this means that sin should be considered harmless and of no real account in the life of the church. The church should be the manifestation in the world of the grace and holiness of God. The church should be the temple of the Holy Spirit. But the sinner makes the form of the church an expression of the evil of her/his heart, giving expression to what is a "den of thieves". So, sin, which certainly has a different relationship to the church than does holiness, is still, nevertheless, a reality that cannot be minimalized.

b. Coping with the Sinful Church

The most fundamental attitude that individual members of the church should have toward the sinful church is recognizing that "sin in the church serves first of all to call to mind our own sinfulness." One is called upon to remember that "our sins are the sins of the church, whether we are priests or laypersons, ... that we all contribute our share to the church's poverty and want".

It is this poverty of the church that brings so clearly into relief the realization that the church "can never place her confidence in her own power and strength but only in God's mercy, which is grace and not merit." Thus, the sinful church reveals the holiness of God, in that "all true holiness is a miracle of God and of grace and not something to be presumptuously taken for granted."

The church is holy exclusively because the church is one with Christ and the Holy Spirit, and this oneness includes distinction as well as inseparability. The church has been founded once and for all until the end of her days by the only Lord. Therefore, if one rejects this church because it does not appear to be the holy church, and consequently becomes a member of a sect, one may indeed be burdened and bothered less by sin and narrowness and scandal. But another consequence is that "perhaps one is nearer to one's ideals, but not nearer to God." In the end, the only certain distinction that can be made in the church is between what is human and what is divine. There is a danger that if one tries to make further distinctions concerning what is human in the church, one may end up excluding what is divine, that is, that which is of the Spirit. The church itself does, to a certain extent, distinguish beyond the distinction of the divine and the human. Thus, to the extent that the church does this, one has the right to do the same. Put in terms of a negative limit, referring to a statement of Pius IX, Rahner repeats that "no one ought to demand more of us than the church, the mother of all, really (and not just presumably) demands of all."

It is true that one can and does encounter sin in the church. But even before one boldly reveals this and responsibly attempts to bring about change, one should first weep, recognizing one's own sins. Rahner calls for a spirituality which bears the form of the church "as virgin and as woman of sin." One should recognize the darker side of the history of the church. But ultimately, one must affirm that "the history of the Spirit of God in the church is still more important and more interesting than the history of human meanness." It is the history of the Spirit of God in the church that points to the "sacred miracle which God daily renews in his church," the miracle that comes about because God has inseparably, yet without confusion, united God's very self to the church, the miracle which consists of the church administering now and always the grace of the sacraments of Christ.[47]

---

[47] Rahner, *Church of Sinners*, p. 268. Unfortunately, the ET completely leaves out the following clause from the section which enumerates what this miracle of the church is in spite of sin: "daß sie jetzt und immer die Gnade der Sakramente Christi verwaltet."

CHAPTER II

VATICAN II PERIOD: ECCLESIOLOGY

Rahner characterized the Second Vatican Council as one which focused upon the church in a unique way: "this Council ... was a Council of the church about the church, a Council in which all the themes discussed were ecclesiological ones, which concentrated upon ecclesiology as no previous Council had ever done."[1] In 1960, Rahner was named consultor to the commission De Sacramentis which did preparatory work for the Council. But it was only in February 1963 that Rahner was officially named as a peritus of the Council and a "member of an expert group of seven theologians who had to work out a new text on the church." The period surrounding Vatican II saw important ecclesiological writings by Rahner.

1. The New Image of the Church

On 3 January 1966, Rahner first gave a lecture in Koblenz (Germany), entitled *The New Image of the Church*. It was a lecture which he would repeat on twelve subsequent occassions between January 3rd and October 25th 1966. The lecture followed by a few weeks the closing of Vatican II on December 8th 1965. It provides an excellent summary and outline of ecclesiological themes which Rahner saw as significant. The lecture serves

---

[1] Rahner, *The New Image of the Church* (hereafter *New Image*) in *TI*, Vol. 10, London, 1973, pp. 3-29, esp. p. 34; first published in *GuL* 39 (1966) 4-24. Rahner concludes that "on an accurate view of the findings of the Second Vatican Council one finds that in all of its sixteen constitutions, decrees and explanations it has been concerned with the church" (p. 3).

to indicate, as well as to highlight, his seven principal ecclesiological positions during the Vatican II period.[2]

a. The Local Community: Church

The Constitution on the church, *Lumen gentium*, as a whole presents the church primarily as a total church, a world church, the unity of all believers in a papally-episcopally constituted association. But Rahner points to the fact that this is not the only possible view to have of the church. He cites *Lumen gentium* itself to support his statement, for the declaration is made there that the church is regarded as church first of all in the local community.[3] And this affirmation, according to Rahner, is the result of a desire for the church to be seen as present as the concrete church of everyday life. The church is more than an abstract ideology, or a dogmatic thesis, or a social mega-organization. The church's true reality is expressed, therefore, in the local community.[4] Thus, even though this perspective, namely, of seeing the church first of all as church in terms of local community, does not permeate every paragraph of *Lumen gentium*, Rahner nevertheless contends that this perspective is present and stated what needed to be stated.[5]

[2] This schema is suggested by M. Fahey, *Decade*, p. 755. Fahey identifies these respectively: 1) that the church is concretely present in the local communities and regional and subordinate churches; 2) that the church is the sacrament of salvation for humanity; 3) the concept of the sinfulness of the church; 4) the church as a communion of faith, hope and love; 5) the church as a charismatic community; 6) the church as gathering of the poor and oppressed; and 7) the church as situated in the eschatological phase of saving history.

[3] Rahner, *New Image*, pp. 8-9. The reference to *LG* is to paragraph 26.

[4] Rahner, *New Image*, p. 8. Rahner uses the terminology *Orts- und Altargemeinde*, = "local and altar community" (ST, Bd. VIII, p. 333). It is clear that he is highlighting the actual assembly of believers and the life of faith which they live. He is stressing this by stating that the church as local community is where the church "celebrates the death of the Lord, breaks the bread of the Word of God, prays, loves and bears the cross of human existence," where the reality of the church is essentially clear and tangible, p. 9.

[5] Rahner, *New Image*, pp. 9-10. Rahner explicitly states that it was impossible to reconstruct the whole of *LG* in light of this perspective of the church as local community.

Rahner is emphatic in declaring that the local community is not a smaller administrative unit of a religious mega-organization. Rather, the local community is the concreteness of the church, and the church only exists as a real, concrete church. Consequently, the concept of the church as a perfect society is not sufficient as a fundamental model of the church.

This concept of the church as perfect society is insufficient for principally two reasons. First, "in and behind the social constitution of the church as a whole, the Spirit, divine truth and love are present and are constantly renewing their vital impact."[6] But secondly, even if one focuses exclusively on the social and juridical structure of the church the concept of the church as perfect society breaks apart. This is so because the whole church is present and realizes itself precisely at the level of proclaiming the word and the level of sacraments. In fact, this is what distinguishes the church from every profane society. This proclamation of the word and sacramental activity occur necessarily on the level of visibility, on the level of that which is socially organized. And this brings to light a major theme in Rahner's theology: "reality in general, and above all, Christian reality is essentially and from its origin a reality to whose self-constitution the 'symbol' necessarily belongs."

It is the concept of church as perfect society that fails to take into consideration this fundamental character of all reality, and consequently of the reality of the church. A fundamental principle of symbolism, as expressed by Rahner, is that the whole is truly present and realizes itself fully in the part. And it is this principle that gives a foundation to Rahner's insistence on the central place in ecclesiology of the local community. In the local community, the whole of the church is present in the part: "the highest truth which can, in the last analysis, be applied to the church as a whole is in fact asserted of the local community itself, namely that in it Christ himself, his gospel, his love and the unity of believers are present."

[6] Rahner, *New Image*, p. 10.

The fundamental difference between the church and the people of God of the Old Testament is seen by affirming the church as church first of all as local community. For the Old Testament people of God actualized or achieved its fullness only through a cumulative process of all the "parts" being brought together. A theological image expressing this is the people of God being gathered together in Jerusalem. The church, on the contrary, can achieve its fullest realization, its deepest actualization, in the local community. This local community appears to be "only a small segment of the church," but, in fact, in this local community is "the most actual and the most intimate presence of Christ."

In a succinct statement, Rahner characterizes an ecclesiology that is rooted in the local community in this way: what happens to the believer in the local community is described not as something occurring in the church, but rather is described as the event of the church itself.[7] Additionally, many aspects of ecclesiology which Rahner believes are going to come into more prominence in the future will necessarily be experienced "first, and by anticipation," in the local community. For the local community is church in the most fundamental and most direct way. This does not mean that the local community can or should be described in any autonomous or isolated fashion. Each local community must give visible expression on the social level to the solidarity and unity with other local communities that are brought about by the Spirit. Therefore, those things which describe the life of the whole church, must naturally also be applicable to the local community.

b. Sacramentum of Salvation of the World

A second significant ecclesiological theme that emerged from Vatican II, according to Rahner, is the affirmation of the Chruch as the *sacramentum* of the salvation of the world. Rahner cautions that the term *sacramentum* is not above all dealing with the constitutional structure of the church. Rather, the concept of the

---

[7] Rahner, *New Image*, p. 121: "event" = *Ereignis*.

church as the basic sacrament of the salvation of the world is one which brings together "two dialectically opposed statements ... to provide a common ground between them." These two positions are: 1) "every human being who acts in good faith according to her/his own conscience attains to the salvation of God in Christ whether s/he is Catholic or not"; [8] and 2) "the church of Christ which finds realisation (*subsistit*) in the Roman Catholic Church, is necessary for salvation (*LG*, 14), is prescribed for all human beings and all human beings for her."

But these two positions must themselves be situated in the context that the church today is concretely a diaspora church, a church that exists in a pluralistic society. It is only from this premise or presupposition that the church as *Grundsakrament* can be properly understood.

At present, and certainly for the foreseebable future, one cannot discern any one church which could be accurately described as the church of all human beings. And so, necessarily, the church as *Grundsakrament* is seen as a reality which points to the grace of God wherever it may occur. To the extent that the grace of God is not visibly, socially and tangibly manifested in its full ecclesial expression, to that extent the church is the *Grundsakrament* of the grace of God wherever that grace occurs. But, at the same time, the grace of God can and does achieve its full ecclesial expression and manifestation in the church. And so the church is *Grundsakrament* also as the actual manifestation of God's grace in its social and historical fullness. There are two extreme positions, both of which Rahner declares are today very much alive, which the concept of the church as *Grundsakrament* is able to counteract. There is the position that all humanity is viewed essentially as massa damnata, and that only those who belong to the church can achieve salvation. And there is the equally extreme position of ecclesiological relativism, which

---

[8] Rahner, *New Image*, p. 12. Such an individual may belong to another Christian confession, or may live according to a non-Christian religion, or may, without culpability, not expressly acknowledge God. Rahner refers to *LG*, paragraph 16.

contends that the church is not so important, because it is only one among many religious groupings. Thus, an individual simply should be free to choose the one that is most appealing.[9]

The relationship of the church as *Grundsakrament* to the salvation of the world is comparable to the relationship of the sacramental word to grace "in the process of salvation which takes place in the life of the individual." Thus, the paradigm of sacrament and grace as it occurs in the life of the individual expresses, in a certain way, the relation of the church to the salvation of the world. And so, precisely, the individual Christian and the church itself must be able to see an actual positive relationship of the church as salvation-reality to the non-ecclesial world. It is in this way that Rahner views the church as the sacrament of the salvation of the world.

The incarnation of the Logos means that the pledge of salvation by God to humanity was not a purely spiritual reality. This pledge of salvation manifests itself above all as a primordial sacramental pledge in Jesus Christ. The historical continuation of Christ's existence, that is, the church, manifests God's pledge as a fundamental-sacramental pledge. And this *grundsakramentale* pledge of grace to the world has an effect on individuals. This *grundsakramentale* pledge of grace ought to be an individual sacramental reality in expressed words and in concrete sacraments, just as the *grundsakramentale* pledge of grace is constituted through the community which receives baptism and celebrates the Lord's Supper. But the self-gift of God's grace can certainly occur in the world beyond those events that are explicitly expressive in word and sacrament of that grace. And wherever such a grace-event occurs, it attains its categorial, salvation-historical tangibility in the church which is seen as *Grundsakrament*. So the church is the "authentic manifestation of grace in history." But the

---

[9] Rahner, *New Image*, p. 13. Rahner contends that ecclesiological relativism is an undercurrent in the faith lives of many Catholic Christians. Such relativism is unacceptable. As Rahner says, the church cannot renounce its absolute character nor its universal mission; for "Christianity is Christ," who is the absolute deed of God's self-gift to humanity.

manifestation of grace in history does not only occur in its full ecclesial expression, that is, in its social visibleness and its ability to be reflected upon verbally.[10]

There are pastoral conclusions that follow from seeing the church as the sacrament of the salvation of the world. First of all, "the Catholic thinks and experiences the church as the 'vanguard,' the sacramental sign, the manifestation in history of a grace of salvation which takes effect far beyond the confines of the 'visible' church as sociologically definable."[11] Also, one is led to consider that non-Christians may be considered as anonymous Christians. Additionally, the faith of the professed Christian "is a grace which once more facilitates and renders more secure precisely that which is already present in the depths of human existence and human awareness, so that it is this that s/he is actually acknowledging by her/his faith." Similarly, one would not maintain a view that the church asserts itself only rarely and with difficulty, nor that the church is simply one of many sects into which humanity has been split, nor that it is simply one of many aspects of a pluralistic society and a pluralistic spirit-life for humanity. Rather, one would affirm that the church manifests itself as a promise to the non-church world. This promise is "the real hope that it will be possible for the world to be redeemed through the church even in those areas of it where its inclusion in the church has not acquired the status of a palpable fact of history."[12]

---

[10] Rahner, *New Image*, p. 14. A serious translation error occurs in the ET, which states: ... "the reality of the church is not only present where it has already fully achieved this status of being explicitly and visibly a social entity, ..." The original indicates that the subject of this sentence is not "the reality of the church," but rather, "the authentic manifestation of grace."

[11] Rahner, *New Image*, pp. 15-16. Rahner explicitly speaks of Christianity which is anonymous, Christianity which exists but "has not realised its true nature, but at the same time is 'within' the church even though it has not achieved its ultimate self-realisation".

[12] Rahner, *New Image*, p. 24.

c. The Sinful Church of Sinners

Rahner admits that even though the theme of the sinful church of sinners may still not have been given the importance in Vatican II that is its due, nevertheless, there has been a significant shift in ecclesiology in this regard. This, too, is an aspect of the new image of the church emerging from Vatican II. "The sinful church of sinners" manifests itself today as an element of ecclesiology much more than an official-ministerial ecclesiology of earlier times was willing to affirm. The picture today is that of the church that must continually be converted to its Lord.

d. Communion of Faith, Hope and Love

The most profound basis for the collegial and synodal principle of the church, which manifested itself so explicitly at Vatican II, is love. The love of those who are in Christ one and the same is specifically the basis, the foundation of all hierarchical distinctions in the church.[13] This unity of love in the Spirit is both the center as well as the goal of the "message of the Gospel and the ministry of the church." Indeed, the love of God and love of neighbor are really one and the same commandment as well as one grace. But the impact which this truth has today in regard to ecclesiology is unsurpassed in comparison with earlier times.

One of the most threatening dangers facing human beings today is the loss of intimacy, the loss of truly personal relationships with others. Not only does this mean that one experiences more a sense of abandonment and loneliness, but that one experiences oneself as a minute, purely functional and replaceable particle of an atom that is related to the huge social reality of today in a mechanical way. It is urgent that everything possible be done to lessen this danger. The church can exercise an important responsibility in this regard.

---

[13] Rahner, *New Image*, p. 24. The ET is not accurate, and at best is confusing. For example, *Differenzierung* is translated as "differences," whereas it should be translated as "distinctions" or "differentiations."

In point of fact, the church must strive to be a community of love in which individuals are able to relate, and are related to, in a way that recognizes the uniqueness of each person. This kind of realization can only occur on the level of the local community. The local church can no longer manifest itself primarily as the manifestation of an institutional mega-organization that provides definitive care of soul-salvation for the individual patient.

Those who hold ministerial office in the church have their authority grounded in "that love that binds together those who are united among themselves as equal, as having been sanctified, and as sharing in community with one another the living experience of the love of Christ."[14] Rahner does not question that there are institutional aspects that necessarily remain in the church, but these have as their foundation this love that unites all. Therefore, the local community cannot be 1) a neighborhood clan with religious trimmings; nor 2) a warm sectarian nest to which the socially frustrated can flee; nor 3) a very holy department store in which an individual can obtain the moral support for one's own individual soul-salvation, while taking notice that there are many other people who are being served in the same department store. It is especially this last approach which contradicts the responsibility of the local community to be first of all a community which enhances personal relationship. Such an approach of collective customer service is very expedient and advisable for meeting individualistic needs. But the local community can and should be a community of love, and love is always something that is extremely concrete. A personal experience of love can only occur in a personal, and not in an anonymous way.

In affirming the local community as a community of love, a serious misconception is overcome that was at times expressed both in the theology of the ancient church writers and in the theology of the Middle Ages. This misconception was that the difference between clergy and laity, or between those in religious

[14] Rahner, *New Image*, p. 26. Rahner notes that in such an environment, "laity and pastors can become accustomed to meet and exchange ideas as members of a family, and it is this that is spoken of in the Constitution on the church (No. 37)."

life and those living as laity, was such that the clergy or those in religious life were ipso facto able to share more deeply in the love of God.[15]

e. Church as Charismatic Community

A characteristic of the church that has been a well-known mark of Rahner's ecclesiology is his highlighting the church as a charismatic community. The church "is not merely the church of hierarchical authorities and of the sacraments, but the church of the free charismata as well."[16]

This theme was treated by Rahner in a foundational manner in 1958.[17] He published three essays dealing with this theme, indicating their inter-relatedness to one another. The first essay argues that there is a "difference in kind ... between principles, which express a universal essence, and prescriptions which are directed to the concrete particular precisely in as much as it is more than an instance of the universal."

The second essay, perhaps more well-known, is entitled *The Charismatic Element in the Church*. The thesis of this essay is closely tied to the first essay. For Rahner concludes that "if in the church there necessarily exists something historically irreducible and unique, and if this arises in the church not by chance but by God, it follows that the church must have a charismatic element." Rahner sees this action of God as having an absolutely unique character with regard to the church and the individual in the church, one which is distinct from the necessary and holy carrying out of principles that are permanently established in the

[15] Rahner, *New Image*, p. 28. There is a very serious translation error in the ET of *TI*. The translation for "die Unterscheidung von Klerus und Laienschaft oder von Ordenstand und Laientum" is given as: "the difference between the clergy and the laity, or between the state of being ordained (sic) and that of not being ordained" (sic). Rahner is indicating that the laity were considered less able to reach holiness than either the clergy or those who belonged to religious orders, that is, religious communities —monastic or otherwise.

[16] Rahner, *New Image*, p. 28. Rahner's reference is to *LG*, 12.

[17] Rahner, *The Dynamic Element in the Church (QD*, 12), New York, 1964 (hereafter *DN*); ET of: *Das Dynamische in der Kirche (QD*, 5), Freiburg, 1958.

church by God. This second essay accordingly treats of "the charismatic element in the church and therefore in the life of the individual member of the church." This has noteworthy significance in regard to ministerial office, particularly with respect to those ordained vis-à-vis those not ordained. For within this essay are treated the topics of the charism of ministerial office (*Amt*) as well as non-institutional charisms, and consequences regarding their relationship to one another and to the church as a whole.

The third essay treats in an epistemological way the question of "how these mysterious concrete particulars in the Christian life of the church are to be known and recognized, if they cannot be inferred from general principles alone." Accordingly, the title of this essay is *The Logic of Concrete Individual Knowledge in Ignatius Loyola*. The essay studies the reality of the guidance by the Holy Spirit of the individual, or, from the other perspective, the reality of the discernment of spirits.

f. Church of the Poor and Oppressed

Today the church is able to recognize itself more than ever before as a church of the poor and the oppressed. The martyrdom of individual members of the church necessarily means that the church experiences martyrdom, that the church suffers, that the church is persecuted.[18] Because the church is made up of individuals who are poor and oppressed, this reality must be affirmed of the church itself.

There are many similarities between this concept of the church and the concept of the church as the sinful church of sinners. In both, it is the living experience of church members that is also predicated of the church itself. The church suffers as an entire church due to the suffering of any one of the church's members who are poor or oppressed in any way.

---

[18] Rahner, *New Image*, p. 28. Rahner notes that the reality of martyrdom is one that is found in non-Catholic churches as well. He cites the pertinent sections in *LG* in regard to seeing the church as the church of the poor and the oppressed, and the reality of martyrdom: *LG*, 8, 41, 42.

g. Pilgrim Church: Eschatology and Ecclesiology

The seventh characteristic that describes for Rahner the new emerging image of the church is that of the pilgrim church. This means that the church is itself "journeying through history to that eternity in which she will cease any longer to be an institution of salvation with an authoritative and sacramental system of this kind." The church waits with sighs for the revelation of the glory of the children of God, for the church is one with all of creation.

The church would understand itself falsely if it were to see itself merely as saving institution, a means of salvation for the individual. Rather, the church realizes itself in its most fundamental way as "the community of those who hope, those who are waiting, of pilgrims who still seek their own homeland, of those who understand and master their present in terms of the future."[19] For in actuality "the church is a means of salvation precisely in so far as she is a community of faith." Therefore, even though the church rightly sees itself as the indicator and the "sacrament of the final salvation which is already present in her ... she ought never to misunderstand herself to the extent of thinking that her present form is the ultimate one. ..."[20] The faith in which the church lives is in the final analysis a faith in a dynamic reality, the dynamic reality of God. And so the faith of the church and of the individual of the church, is fundamentally an eschatological faith which looks to the future for its fulfillment. Salvation is fundamentally an "event which is now already taking place but is not yet finished."

[19] Rahner, *The Church and the Parousia of Christ* (hereafter *Parousia*) in *TI*, Vol. 6, London, 1969, pp. 295-312, esp. p. 297. First published in *Cath* 17 (1963) 113-128.

[20] Rahner, *Parousia*, p. 297. The church cannot ignore the fact that it has its own history. And that history is experienced as both an ongoing development or unfolding of the church, as well as an experience of "growing old." Thus, a true development "signifies at the same time a symptom of old age, the danger of losing herself in details and matters of secondary importance or in a too self-reliant entrenchment in this aeon" (n. 2, pp. 297-298).

The church's relationship to history is important to understand. The church, in the context of history, both hears God's word of grace and is this word of grace. But even the word of grace which the church is in a permanent and indestructible way, occurs in a real, actual, historical form which changes. Consequently, the church must not fail to recognize itself in its provisional character. For since the church exists in history, the church, as a historical church, is progressively moving toward the parousia where all history will be eliminated. [21]

Yet, the church as an eschatological reality has a different relationship to history than other created realities. For the church cannot be seen as a "purely external religion organisation." The church in its members is actually graced by the Spirit of Christ, and this reality of the Spirit "is one of the most essential constitutive elements of the church."

This reality of the church follows clearly from Rahner's theology of grace. For he sees that God's grace, that is, the self-communication of God to human beings, is an event that takes place "even now," and is not simply a future event that is merely promised for human beings at a later time. He succinctly declares: "the doctrine of grace, at least in the Catholic understanding of it, states that God is in his self-communication the principle of the movement to the goal which is himself." [22] Therefore, the church which realizes the acceptance of the offer of God's grace, belongs to this eschatological reality itself.

Rahner affirms that the self-communication of God to human beings is victorious, because not only God's offer, but also the free acceptance by human beings of God's offer is itself realized by the grace of God. Jesus, as fully human, is the foundation of that victory. The church, for its part, "lends to this victory an historical and in a certain sense sacramental presence and tangibility in the world." Therefore, the church is not merely pro-

---

[21] Rahner, *Parousia*, p. 298. Thus, the provisional character of the church does not consist in the fact that the church will be abolished by history, but that history itself will be abolished.

[22] Rahner, *Parousia*, p. 300, n. 4.

claiming a victory on God's part in which the church has not yet shared. Rather, the very proclamation of the church is that the church is the historical presence of this victory. Therefore, to the extent that the church is the actual historical presence of the victory of God, the church will never perish. Looked at positively, one necessarily affirms of the church an indefectibility of its holiness and its faith.

Rahner considers specifically the nature of the relationship between the reality of the church's indefectibility and the official ministry of the church. He states that the eschatological character of the church follows from understanding the church as the fruit of salvation as contrasted with the church understood as means of salvation. Therefore, what is the relationship between the church as an eschatological reality and the institutional aspect of the church as particularly seen in its official ministry?

First, it is necessary to affirm that ministerial office in the church cannot be absolutely identified, in a Donatist fashion, with the church as grace. Yet, Rahner states that there is an indefectibility of the church in its institutional office, and this indefectibility, indeed, follows from understanding the church as the fruit of salvation. This indefectibility of the ministerial office is necessarily rooted in the church's union with Christ. Christ and the church are essentially inseparable but at the same time are not absolutely identified. Therefore, if one is to affirm this permanent union between Christ and the church, then the official ministry of the church must be such that it never separates the church as a whole from Christ. For this ministerial office is founded by Christ as an authoritative dimension in the church on which the faith, the worship and the action of the community depend and must depend.[23] Therefore, if the community were separated from its

---

[23] Rahner, *Parousia*, p. 307. Additionally, in a clarifying note, Rahner states: "In saying this we are not denying that an ultimate indefectibility of the church's official ministry can be derived from those texts of the New Testament which speak directly about the church's office, of its mission and its function within the church. But if the question is then asked why such an indefectibility belongs to this office in the New Covenant although no such indefectibility ever belonged to any

own ministerial office, the community of salvation would no longer be, at least in the dimension of its historical tangibility, the historical presence and tangibility of the victory of the grace of Christ.

This indicates, as well, the limits regarding the understanding of the indefectibility of ministerial office in the church. Ministerial office in the church, its teaching, sanctifying, and pastoral power, "participates in the indefectibility of the community of salvation if and in so far as it would, were it not itself indefectible, in safeguarding the structure of the church, tear her away from Christ so that the church as an historical phenomenon would cease to be the eschatologically indefectible community of salvation." Consequently, those acts "which do not possess this indefectibility necessarily and inevitably belong to her pilgrim existence in faith and hope." And this expresses the reality that the church is a pilgrim church, and a church that must be tempted and challenged by its own pilgrim existence. Only in this way can the church be a community of faith and hope.

Rahner notes that, unfortunately, too often little or no attention is given to the fact that the church realizes itself both in a defectible as well as an indefectible way. And this is necessarily true of the church's ministerial office. The key point, particularly in terms of its consequences for ecumenism, is that it is not possible to reflect subsequently and to make an absolutely clear separation between what is defectible and indefectible in the church.[24] If this were emphasized more clearly, a false image of

office up to then in the history of salvation in spite of it being positively led and guided by God, even when that office was bestowed by God himself, then the only possible answer is that here it is a question of an office in a church which is itself the eschatological fruit of salvation and as such (but only as such) cannot be other than indefectible" (n. 6, p. 306).

[24] Rahner, *Parousia*, p. 308. Rahner notes that both aspects of the reality of church must be affirmed. He also points out that all too often only the reality of indefectibility with respect to the teaching ministerial office of the church is looked at. Consequently, those instances of indefectibility on the part of the teaching ministerial office, that is, those realities identified as infallible, are seen as establishing the norm. That which is non-infallible is seen to be of little value and

the church could be done away with, or at least minimized: the image of the church and individual members who "wander idly from one clear certitude to another." Such an image obscures or can even deny the fundamental reality for the church and for the individual member, namely, that one can "trust in the grace of God alone." Trusting in the grace of God alone is, what may be called, the bottom line. For it is not possible to ascertain with certainty some "pure" and "untarnished" part of the church upon which one can rely with absolute certainty and total confidence. The church community, and therefore the individual member, lives ultimately a life of faith and hope in the love of God.

Rahner offers a final consideration with regard to the topic of ecclesiology and eschatology. He points to a new reality which did not exist in previous times. Today, human beings are able to change and fashion the world as they choose. In past times, human beings were able to respond to the world around them in principally two ways: surrender or protest, or frequently some combination of these two. But now human beings assume a much more creative and active role in the created world. Therefore, Rahner sees the challenge as this: "The church as the eschatological community of salvation living in the faith and the hope of a future which is the gift of God himself and which is not designed and created by human beings, must come to terms with this new existential experience of the modern human being to whom is opened both for her/himself as an individual and for humanity as a whole a real and extensive future which can be foreseen, planned, and realised."

In recent history, since the beginnings of this new reality, the attitude of the church has frequently been an attitude of criticism rather than support. Rahner clearly states that if the church wants to exercise influence or offer guidance to humanity today,

---

consequence. What Rahner emphasizes is the importance of recognizing how indefectibility is a reality of each aspect of the church's ministerial office, namely its teaching, sanctifying, and pastoral ministerial office.

then the church must not only recognize that this new reality on the part of humanity is legitimate, but that it is part of the over-all plan of God. In fact, the active and creative involvement of humanity in fashioning creation is radically Christian. Thus, by affirming the legitimacy and the necessity of this new reality, the church can then state its belief that this new future itself "is redeemed and sanctified and given its proper meaning ... in the kairos of Christ." The church will not be the "true and eschatolo-gical community of salvation" if the church is "resentful, ineffec-tual, and fearful" in its attitude. The world must be valued and accepted precisely in its profane worldliness, "without again sublimating its worldliness in a religious sense." This new reality is not something that the church can afford to ignore. If the church's attitude toward this new reality is not one first of all of acceptance, but rather of indifference or rejection, the church's own understanding of itself as the eschatological salvation-community will be misinterpreted by the church itself and will be misunderstood by non-Christians.

2. Church and World

Although published in 1968, the article by Rahner in SM entitled *Church and World* can be considered a conclusion to the Vatican II period of his ecclesiological writings.[25] In this article Rahner presents reflections not offered elsewhere on the relation-ship of church and world as seen from the perspective of Vatican II. Thematically, these reflections are closely related to concepts and views that Rahner deals with in regard to questions of ecclesiology and eschatology.

Rahner notes that while the church has always been concerned with the theme of its relationship with the world, today the question is markedly different than in past times. It is literally a question of the relationship of the church with the world itself, and specifically, says Rahner, "a world which is not simply an

---

[25] Rahner, *Church and World* in *SM*, Vol. 1, London, 1968, pp. 346-357.

antecedent datum, a situation of interest solely in the perspective
of salvation. It is a world planned and produced by humanity
itself and it therefore concerns humanity even in its own empirically observable importance." Three aspects that significantly
affect the relation of the church to the world are: 1) the reality of
a divided Christendom; 2) the reality of many non-Christian
religions; and 3) the reality that in a pluralist society the State has
a function quite different from its task in an "ideologically
homogeneous society."

a. Fundamental Understanding of World

The term "world" has, for Rahner, three distinct theological
meanings: 1) "the good created world"; 2) "the sinful world of
perdition"; and 3) "the redeemed world oriented supernaturally
by grace which is the situation in which salvation is worked out."
All three of these meanings are linked together by the fact that
the world is history and is not simply an "unchanging stage" on
which history acts out its part. Consequent to recognizing that
the world is history, Rahner affirms that the world is a "unity in
multiplicity" (Einheit und Differenz) which can never be adequately done away with. He states that "while Christianity recognizes
a certain dualism between God and world in redemptive history,
a dualism which is already in process of dissolution, it does not
acknowledge any radical and insuperable dualism." For while the
world is in need of redemption, it is also capable of being
redeemed. This presents the Christian with a task, the task, made
possible by grace, to discern how this development can take
place, "while critically distinguishing the forces present in it (the
sinful world) and patiently bearing its burden and darkness which
will never cease until the end."

b. Fundamental Understanding of Church

The term "church" must also be understood in its meaning.
Rahner insists that the church "is not identical with the kingdom
of God." Rather, it is the salvation-historical sacrament of the

kingdom of God. It is situated in the eschatological phase of salvation history in which the kingdom of God occurs —for it must occur in history if it is to have significance for human beings— but it does not occur definitively until the "coming of Christ and the last judgment."

There is also another way in which the kingdom of God and the church cannot be identified. The church is the "socially constituted, historically visible society (*Gemeinschaft!*; more exactly translated: "community" or "communion") of the redeemed." But the kingdom of God comes to be "wherever obedience to God occurs in grace as the acceptance of God's self-communication". And this acceptance always has a categorical dimension, and may be realized, for example, "in the concrete fulfillment of an earthly task, of active love of others, even of collective love of others." Yet, even such an occurrence of grace will always retain a certain ambiguity in its ability to be observed. Grace remains, to a certain extent, "hidden."

The kingdom of God cannot be absolutely identified with any worldly reality, and it must be recognized that the church is indeed in the world and that its members bring about world history. Therefore, Rahner understands the term church in its truest sense as the specific fundamental sacrament which manifests that "in the unity, activity, fraternity, etc. of the world, the kingdom of God is at hand." And he adds the caveat, that just as is true regarding the individual sacraments, so specifically in affirming the church as *Grundsakrament*, "sign and thing signified can never be separated or identified."

c. History: Context of the Relation of Church and World

The relationship between the church and the world is grounded in the fact that there is not only a profane history of the world, but the church itself is led in an "historical process under the guidance of the Holy Spirit." Their mutual relationship itself is therefore capable of change, and actually does change. In addition, the church in its ministerial office, but even more clearly in all its members, is imperfect, and may even be sinful. Therefore, this can "distort and falsely determine" the relationship between the church and the world.[26]

Rahner stresses that the church is necessarily rooted in the historical. This does not contradict, in Rahner's eyes, the fact that the church has been entrusted with the fullness of truth. For he declares that "the church itself is only slowly led into the fullness of truth which it already possesses." And he illustrates this process by pointing to some examples.[27] Furthermore, the changes that do come about in the church are changes that are made in conformity with the truth and spirit of the church itself, and are not simply an adaptation to something that the church is powerless to change.[28]

If one respects the historical character of the relationship of the church and world, then it is important to recognize, says Rahner, that this relation "always has to be determined anew in the concrete." It is not possible to establish once and for all how church and world relate to one another. Equally important is the recognition that human decisions regarding the relation of church and world are themselves "original" in the sense that such

[26] Rahner, *Church and World*, p. 348. This can occur, for example, "through one's trespassing on the domain of the other, through neglect or misinterpretation of the function which each in its own way can and should perform for the other."

[27] Rahner, *Church and World*, p. 348: 1) the church only slowly learns fully to appreciate the freedom of the individual and of human groups; 2) to value the unity and multiplicity of the many churches which the one church comprises and also their basis in national and secular history (cf. Vatican II: Decrees on Eastern Catholic churches and on Ecumenism); 3) the church only slowly came to acknowledge the relative autonomy of the secular sciences; 4) the potential variety of the social, political, and economic organization of human groups (decline of mistrust of democracy or of certain forms of socialization etc.); 5) the church is slowly attaining a more unconstrained, comprehensive and personal appreciation of human sexuality.

[28] Rahner, *Church and World*, p. 349. For example, Rahner believes that the "change in the Western mind in modern times ultimately sprang from the spirit of Christianity itself, even though it often rightly or wrongly turned against the actual existing church and forced it slowly to learn what it really always knew. That change led from a Greek cosmocentrism to anthropocentrism, (it) meant destroying the numinous character of the world and making it the material of human activity."

decisions cannot be simply deduced from eternal principles. Therefore, it is always a struggle to determine this relation. Rahner
expresses it specifically as a relation that is dialectical and that is
constantly changing; its two poles are: 1) flight from the world;
and 2) affirmation of the world. And so, in this dialectical process,
the church comes to realize itself as "not of this world," but also as
"the sacrament of the absolute future of the world."

d. Integrism: An Ecclesiological Heresy

Following a method upon which he relies often, Rahner sket-
ches two fundamental ways in which the relation of the church
and world are wrongly conceived. The first of these heresies he
names "Integrism"; the second he calls "Esotericism".

The heresy of integrism has important significance in studying
the relationship between church and ministerial office due to its
basic premise: that the official ministerial church can fully suc-
ceed in achieving a synthesis between the church and the world,
that it can accomplish in history that which others view as being
the asymptotic goal that is beyond history. Following from this
premise is the conviction of integrism that anything that is of
importance for salvation necessarily belongs to the official ministerial church.

In effect, what integrism does is declare the world to be
"corpus christianum and nothing else." The world is to be fully
integrated into the church. The assumption upon which the basic
premise of integrism is based is that the official ministerial church,
through its pastoral ministerial office, is able clearly and compre-
hensively to determine all particular, concrete, moral actions of
human beings. These, it believes, can be deduced from the
principles that are defended by the church. Others only need to
put into practice what the church teaches and expounds. This
assumption, declares Rahner, is false: "It is not possible wholly
to derive from the principles of natural law and the gospel the
human action which ought to be done here and now, although of
course all action must respect these principles." Rahner insists

that the action of individuals which is more than the carrying out of the principles expounded by the church is itself concerned with salvation and must be carried out with moral responsibility. Similarly, charismatic action is possible, that is, action from on high which does not originate or have its basis in the official ministerial church. This action, without its being or becoming ecclesial, that is, while remaining of the world, shares in the coming of the kingdom of God.

It is important for human beings to try to integrate and synthesize the multiplicity of experiences and impulses and the situations of "concupiscence" to which they are exposed. But this pluralism is an intrinsic reality for the human being which can never be completely overcome. Integrism believes otherwise.

Rahner seems to indicate how ironic it is that the heresy of integrism is a particular danger today because the world is moving from a static condition to a more dynamic one. Integrism thus may have significant impact in manipulating and altering the future according to its approach to the world. But the very condition which allows integrism to have such impact espouses the opposite stance from integrism: "that the actively created future is no longer to be deduced from eternal principles." Though Rahner does not make this link explicitly, it would seem quite justifiable to see many of the elements that he identifies in integrism occurring in biblical —and other— fundamentalism.

Finally, Rahner sees an important consequence that results from a repudiation of integrism: the layperson in the church, particularly in her/his world task, is much more than someone who simply receives directions from the official ministerial church. And, even when the layperson is not explicitly carrying out an action that has its origin in the official ministerial church, the individual layperson continues to act specifically as a Christian in realizing responsible, historical decisions. Rahner's summary statement is clear: "action regulated by the church and Christian action which is genuinely human do not coincide."

e. Esotericism: An Opposite Ecclesiological Heresy

The heresy of esotericism declares that the only genuine Christian attitude toward the world is flight from the world. Any positive relation of church to world is highly suspect. The things that are of this world are judged —at best— as indifferent in relation to the church.

Esotericism, which has many sources and takes on different appearances, is an undialectical attitude. It may be rooted, for example, in a dualism which identifies the empirical world with its sinfulness, believing that the more one distances oneself from the world, the more one distances oneself from sin, and, consequently, the closer one draws to God. Thus, esotericism can judge itself as thoroughly Christian.[29]

One variety of esotericism can be a part of the belief system of those who see the church primarily or exclusively as an invisible church whose predestined members are known only to God. Such an ecclesiology is meta-historical. This attitude becomes incarnate, so to speak, in the Catholic tradition in the view that "life according to the evangelical counsels in the religious orders is of itself the sole or self-evidently the higher realization of the Christian spirit from which the many are dispensed only because of their weakness."

It is possible for both integrism and esotericism to constitute together a particular approach or life style. This, notes Rahner, is what occured in the Irish monastic church, which sought "to make the world a monastery." But in viewing esotericism in itself, its "decisive feature" is that the things of the world are abandoned to themselves, recognized as indifferent at best, and more

---

[29] Rahner, *Church and World*, p. 350. It can claim to be in conformity with, among other things: 1) the NT attitude of the Sermon on the Mount; 2) the recommendation of sexual abstinence; 3) indifference to social conditions; 4) imminent expectation of the end of the world, etc. On that basis it may consider that all Christian life has in this NT attitude not only an ever necessary warning and correction but its total expression, and all that has to be done is simply to maintain and reproduce this.

often, clearly sinful. The world presents no positive task to the
"esoteric" Christian.

Having identified the (heretical) approaches of intergrism and
esotericism, Rahner declares that a "true relation of the Christian
and the church to the world lies in the mean between these two
extremes." And this mean should not be seen as a forced compro-
mise on the part of the Christian and the church. Rather, it is an
approach that combines into a radical unity "both the unity of
what is explicitly Christian and ecclesiastical on the one hand,
and the world and secular action on the other." Furthermore, the
relation of the church and world to one another must be seen in a
two-fold way. On the one hand, there is the relationship of the
official ministerial church to the world. On the other hand, there
is the relationship of Christians, especially the laity, to the world,
"for all of them also are (*bilden*; more exactly: 'form' or 'make'),
of course, the church."

f. The Relation of Church (Amtskirche) and World

The official ministerial church must "renounce all integrism
even merely in practice." The church, because it is an historically,
juridically constituted society will always have institutional relations with the world.[30] It is to be expected, therefore, that the
church has a "certain social power". Nonetheless, Rahner believes
that this is decreasing due to the fact that the church is becoming
more and more a diaspora church.[31] But the important point for
the church to guard against, says Rahner, is to not use whatever
social power it has —and as an institution it will always have

[30] Rahner, *Church and World*, p. 351. For example, Rahner recognizes that
concordats may still be possible and useful means for "regulating relationships
between church and world," though he is of the opinion that such methods may be
found less effective in the future. He also sees it acceptable for the church to have
diplomatic representatives, and that the church can seek recognition of its church
schools and educational systems where good ones can be realized.

[31] Rahner, *Church and World*, p. 352. Rahner identifies this transition as
moving from the experience of a "popular" church (*Volkskirche*) to a church of
professed believers. The ET of *Volkskirche* as "national church" is inexact and
very misleading terminology.

some social power— as a "means of exerting pressure in order to attain its legitimate aims." For this would be a betrayal on the part of the church in that it settles for something less than "human beings' free, unforced obedience in a faith which has perpetually to be exercised anew." The church must not use any worldly means of coercion against its own baptized members. Its attitude must reveal above all else that it seeks to be "a socially constituted community of those who freely believe in Christ, ... that it is not the religious institution of a State or of a secular society as such."[32] The result of this is that the church will not appear so much as a traditional, almost folkloric institution that is maintained to offer religious customs to children whose Catholic parents have had them baptized.

An even more significant result of the church being primarily a community of freely professed believers is that the church can be much more a missionary church. It can honestly seek adults to be baptized, whose lives and personalities have already been formed in positive ways outside the church.

One final responsibility on the part of the official ministerial church is to free individual Christians from the misconception that one's moral decision is in conformity with God's will "by the mere fact that it does not come into conflict with the material content of the church's norms." Rahner describes this necessary attitude of the official ministerial church as an attitude of liberating modesty. It is an attitude by which the church encourages that which is truly Christian even though it will occur outside the limits of the visibly, juridically constituted church.

g. The Relation of Church (Volk Gottes) and World

The relationship to the world of individual Christians as members of the church, that is, the church as people of God, is partly different from the relationship to the world of the official ministerial church. This relationship of the Christian to the world is

---

[32] Rahner, *Church and World*, p. 352.

determined fundamentally by the fact of the Incarnation. For it is in the Incarnation that God's acceptance of the world takes place. Acceptance of the world by God "means the setting free of the world into independence, intrinsic significance and autonomy".

There are two related but distinct realities concerning this setting free of the world. On the one hand, this is an emancipation that takes place in history; it can become "fuller and clearer" in the course of history. Rahner notes that this has indeed happened. On the other hand, this "freed world" in its independence and autonomy is at the same time a masking or a veiling of the acceptance of the world by God. The world does not give an unambiguous confirmation that it has been freed by God. This is something that only faith and hope can discern.

This last point is a very important one for Rahner. He emphasizes that the world, truly emancipated by God, "does not simply move in an evolutionary way towards its integration into the love of God, into his epiphany in the world and into the kingdom of God." Rather, this development takes place without abolishing the "concupiscent" aspect of the world. Consequently, this "historical growth" takes place through "collapse, futility, the zero of death". It is this reality of the "concupiscence" of the world that is both the "manifestation of the sin of the world' and the mediation and manifestation of the redemptive sharing in Christ's lot". In fact, the world, "precisely in its concupiscent secular nature," is the world which has been "accepted by God in Christ."

For Rahner, it is the meaning of the saving cross that allows the Christian to understand this "concupiscent secularity." The world cannot be viewed as Christian only insofar as it is integrated or interpreted in an explicitly religious and ecclesial way. It is not possible for there to be such a completely "successful" integration or interpretation. Therefore, the Christian is not only justified but required to "calmly (*unbefangen*; more exactly: "impartially") be secular, and have earthly wishes and goals and enjoy the empirical world without religious mediation." Such an attitude can be understood spontaneously as the way in which one obediently entrusts oneself to the decrees of God which are not able simply to be at the disposal of a person. This is exemplified particularly in one's readiness to accept the frustration or futility of the world as well as to accept death itself.

Rahner concludes that "the earthly task and the 'heavenly' vocation" must be distinguished and differentiated from each other, but understood in such a way that does not destroy their unity —which is the heresy of esotericism— nor declare that they are simply identical —which is the heresy of integrism. It would not seem presumptive to recognize here Rahner's often-repeated Chalcedonian Christological position that the humanity and divinity of Christ are neither confused nor separate with respect to one another.

h. Church: Sacrament of the Salvation of the World

Similarly, the relation between "the earthly task and the heavenly vocation" cannot be unambiguously determined in the concrete. And so, in the church, this relationship can only be, and, in fact, must be fully manifested by recognizing two elements which rightly describe the church as a whole. On the one hand, the church is church as the people of God. And on the other hand, the church is church as the sacrament of the salvation of the world. Every individual in the church has a different call and task that must be placed in the context of these two concepts of the church.

1° Flight from the World

Thus, one recognizes that there is rightly and necessarily in the church what can be described as "flight from the world".[33] But this flight from the world can be properly understood only within the context of affirming the church not only as "people of God," but also as "sacrament of the salvation of the world." Any

---

[33] Rahner, *Church and World*, p. 354. More particularly, Rahner notes this as: "asceticism, flight from the world, the life of the evangelical counsels as imitation of the Crucified and as inchoative advance towards that renunciation of the world which is demanded of everyone in death, and the life of the religious orders".

ascetical practice cannot be appreciated simply as "a well-tried method of combatting sin and its threat," but must also be seen as the "sign in the church for the church and the world that the world is the world of God, of grace, of hope in the absolute future of God, which God himself bestows and which is not simply identical with the autonomous development of the world." If any type of flight from the world fails to affirm its service as a sign function in the church, then it becomes un-Christian. "Legitimate flight from the world is an exercise of faith and hope in the divinely bestowed fulfillment of the world and consequently a sign of that courage of faith which can serenely allow the world to be the world, that is, finite." A legitimate Christian flight from the world can never intend to be something that is complete. Rather, it occurs in the life of a Christian together with a decision to "take the world seriously." A Christian can enjoy the world because God has given himself to the world as the ultimate content of the world's significance so that it "may be free and independent."

2° Ministry to the World

The gift of God's self to the world is also the foundation for a ministry to the world in the church. Such a ministry to the world is, on the part of the church, being responsible for the world. It means an "acceptance" of the (*Sicheinlassen*; perhaps better and more forcefully translated: "a getting involved with the") secularity of the world, and an intention for the unfolding of all those dimensions which, through human beings, exist in the world.

What is at the heart of understanding Rahner's views about the church's ministry to the world is his affirmation that on the one hand the secular is "opened out towards God by the grace of God." Christian ministry to the world does not have its beginnings simply when something is done out of explicit Christian motivation, or simply when that which is "profane" is re-shaped by theology into something that is "Christian." Rahner describes life that is lived with this recognition as world-Christian life, which, at times, may be lived in an anonymously Christian way.

On the other hand, that which is Christian affirms that although the world is opened towards God by the grace of God, the world is not identified with God. And so, to those who are living lives that Rahner describes as Christian-world lives, there belongs not only an enjoyment of the world and its activities, but also a readiness for death (with Christ), "the Spirit of the Sermon on the Mount, of the evangelical counsels, the practice of readiness for renunciation," and a "skepticism in regard to any identification with the world that would make an absolute of the world and idolize it, i.e., identify it ultimately with God."

What is crucial, and always for the individual, is how to unite flight from the world with activity in the world. Such a unity can only be achieved if it is a reality that is always individually oriented, both respecting and being determined by the unique "vocation" of the particular individual, and the individual's own spiritual experience.

For the church to be the sacrament of the salvation of the world, the church must be able to be described as fleeing from the world —and consequently able to be critical of the world— and at the same time as a church that adheres to the world. The church must manifest this in a variety of ways and serve in a way that is reciprocal and mutual among those who each have a unique vocation. For the world, for which the church is the sacrament of salvation, itself should exist and grow.

These two realities of fleeing from the world and adhering to the world are related to one another in a dialectical way. Rahner has great confidence that there is no reason to worry or be mistrustful about the relation of the church and the world as long as both elements are present in the church. The fact that the world today possesses a character that is dynamic, as contrasted with a much more static concept in the past, means that the church must willingly accept new, emerging tasks in which it can engage in regard to its ministry to the world. The more static concept of the world often brought about a much more cautious attitude on the part of the church. It was based on an approach that did not want to concede anything to the spirit of the world

—judged to be significantly evil. Such a static concept engendered a fear of being contaminated by the worldliness —used in a pejorative sense— of the world. But the dynamic concept of today's world calls forth from the church a responsibility to take part in helping to fashion and create this world. It is a challenge from which the church cannot turn away.

Conclusion

There are four areas that Rahner indicates as significant in regard to the relationship of church and world. They are of differing relevance and import.

First, he sees it as imperative that the church as a whole church (*Gesamtkirche*) has tasks that relate directly to the fact that the world today is more and more a single world. Consequently, he recognizes that the church as a whole church needs to organize itself appropriately in order to undertake responsible tasks benefiting the development of the world as a single world, which continues to realize itself in this way more and more.

Secondly, if the church on the one hand must be necessarily everywhere in this single world, but, on the other hand be a church which is always the "sign which is contradicted," the church consequently will be "a diaspora-church in a pluralist world." A consequence that follows from this is that the church must have the courage to make the transition from a church that is a "popular" church (*Volkskirche*) to a church that is a community church (*Gemeindekirche*). A "popular" church is characterized by what Rahner describes as an entire people, or at least a significant portion of a people, being a part of "traditional church-membership". Contrasted with this is a community church which is characterized by those who (generally smaller in number) personally believe by their own decision.

A point of particular interest is Rahner's conviction that this transition to the church as community necessarily means a church of "open dialogue with the world." This dialogue with the world occurs as an inner-oriented dialogue with the world "inside" the church itself, as well as an outer-oriented dialogue with the world "outside" the church.

For the church as community, without ceasing to exist with a hierarchical structure, "is based on the laity as personal believers, and less on the institutional element and its power in society or on the clergy as the traditional supports and recipients of its social prestige."[34] Rahner, therefore, notes that such a laity is ipso facto the world in the church. But that the clergy as well, whom Rahner describes as being "of our time," join together with the laity in bringing into the church an already existing "culture, mentality, endeavors, etc... . (which) are no longer created solely by the church as an institution (as was almost entirely the case in earlier times)."[35] Consequently, an inner-oriented dialogue of the church with the world is based on this reality.

There also exists an outer-oriented dialogue of the church with the world. This is because the church as community, inevitably as a diaspora-church, cannot be sectarian, but rather must be fundamentally missionary. To be missionary it must be in open dialogue with the world's cultures, endeavors, and creations, and not live in a ghetto mentality, affirming only what it designates, for example, as "Christian literature," or "Christian art." The fundamental principle that must be respected to enable the church to be missionary is: the church must be willing to receive, in order to be able to give.

Rahner's third point focuses on the reality of the cross. He believes that there are elements of today's situation that the church cannot naively believe are simply temporary, such as: 1) the impersonably organized mass society of today; 2) a "profane" culture; 3) a relative lack of any expressiveness of what is Christian in the present time; and 4) the diaspora situation of the church. Since the church cannot reasonably expect these realities to disappear, Rahner recognizes in them a significance drawn

[34] Rahner, *Church and World*, p. 355.
[35] Rahner, *Church and World*, pp. 355-356. Bestrebungen: "endeavors" is wrongly translated as "aspirations" in the ET.

from the cross. He expresses it in this way: "we have to endure the sober harshness of an unromantic, planned technical world with all the burdens which such a situation brings upon itself and Christianity." He speaks of this reality as a part of the cross not because the cross itself should be sought after. Rather, to seek to avoid the cross in this case would lead to choosing one of two extremes. On the one hand, the church is tempted to adopt an attitude of "reactionary resistance to the approaching future." On the other hand, the church is tempted to choose an "eschatologism which instead of sober waiting for the Lord would mean a flight forward impelled by what in fact would be an ideology of this world."

The plea that Rahner makes is thus for the church to give up the attitude that so clearly describes the church in the Medieval period: "a very direct and universal control of all human realities." If the church heeds this plea, it does not mean that a Christian would cease to fashion the world in as Christian a way as possible. It would mean, rather, that a Christian would be more sensitive to the fact that God's grace is everywhere, and that consequently, it is possible that a particular "Christian" way of fashioning the world may first be realized by a non-Christian. A Christian would also be more aware that the simple fact that one is an explicit Christian does not necessarily mean that one will always shape the world in a Christian way.

Rahner's fourth and final point is fundamentally a reassertion that a decision by the church not to exercise "a direct and universal control over all human realities" is not a decision to flee into what would be a utopia, or to the comfortable and secure, or into the sacristy. Rather, the church's shift is rightly based on a deeper understanding of its own self. The church is not a "world-organization ... for a better world —on earth." It is, rather, the "community of believers in that eternal life in God, into which history is raised and transcended."[36]

[36] Rahner, *Church and World*, p. 356. Rahner adds that "only in the measure in which the church is the 'kingdom not of this world' does it in the long run hold the promise that it is the blessing of eternity for time."

CHAPTER III

LATER ECCLESIOLOGICAL WRITINGS

The final fifteen years of Rahner's life continue to be marked by ecclesiological concerns. His theological writings during this period, specifically on ecclesiological themes, often arise as a response to realities that he observes in and about the church. Three particular events have been identified as having a significant relation to his ecclesiological writings of this period.

First was his involvement in the West German Pastoral Synod, which took place from 1971-1975. The beginning of the Synod coincided with Rahner's decision to retire from his teaching position at Münster 3 September 1971. The event of the Synod moved him into closer contact with the "average German Catholic" and local parishes enabling him "to understand better the aspirations and frustrations" in the church that were occuring. An important ecclesiological work was occasioned by the Synod, *The Shape of the Church to Come*.[1]

Rahner's membership in the Vatican's International Theological Commission from 1969 to 1974 was the second factor that had an influence on his writings on ecclesiological themes. This contact gave him a much wider perspective regarding the reality of the church.

A third factor to have an influence on his writings during this period was his moving from Münster, upon his retirement, to Munich, and subsequently to Innsbruck.[2] Rahner died at Inns-

---

[1] Rahner, *The Shape of the Church to Come* (hereafter *Shape*), London, 1974. The original German was first published in November, 1972. H. Vorgrimler, *Understanding Karl Rahner*, London, 1986, p. 109, states that Rahner's work raised three questions: 1) Where do we stand? 2) What should we do? and 3) How do we conceive of a church of the Future?

[2] M. Fahey, *Decade*, p. 756. Fahey notes that during this period Rahner "developed considerable interest in the phenomenon of basic Christian communi-

bruck on 30 March 1984, just a few weeks following the celebration of his 80th birthday on 5 March.

The theological writings of this last period of Rahner's life are
marked with a particular distinctiveness. Leo O'Donovan offers
an overview of this period and describes the writings "with their
bold and unrepressed fidelity to tradition, their restless yet serene
spirituality, their sometimes even angry love."[3] The ecclesiological writings alone of this period manifest the enormous breadth
of interest on Rahner's part. My own focus here is to look at
these writings as they relate to the understanding of Rahner's
sacramentology of ministry.

1. Anthropological Ecclesiology

"The church," says Rahner, "is neither an idea nor a principle
nor a postulate". The church, rather, must be described as a
'visible' church, as the concrete 'people of God,' as a "social
entity," a "formal group," an "institution in the world." The
temptation which must be resisted is that of seeing the church
exclusively or predominantly in terms only of its nature (*ius
divinum*), which consequently hides from the church its "real
concrete reality". In other words, the image of what the church
should be hinders one from recognizing the church as it is.[4]

a. People of God — People of the Church

Rahner notes that the Vatican II Constitution on the church,
Lumen gentium, accurately presents the "essential structure of the
people of God which is the church." But he contends that there is
more that needs to be said which goes beyond, without elimina-

---

ties (*Basisgemeinden*)." See, in this regard, Rahner, *Basic Communities* in *TI*, Vol.
19, London, 1984, pp. 159-165.

[3] L. O'Donovan, *A Journey into Time: The Legacy of Karl Rahner's Last
Years*, in *TS* 46 (1985) p. 624.

[4] Rahner, *On the Structure of the People of the Church Today* (hereafter
Structure) in *TI*, Vol. 12, London, 1974, pp. 218-228, esp. p. 218.

ting, what Vatican II has said concerning the church. He presents the distinction in terminology between the "people of God" and the "people of the church". These are not identical concepts. Rahner uses the term people of the church to emphasize that there can be no ecclesiological monophysitism in the church. His point is that "the human factor, including therefore the social life of human beings ... is —'undivided and unmixed'— an intrinsic element in the church itself." Therefore, he concludes that it is essential to make use of "secular sociological categories and models" to accurately describe the "structures of the people of the church."

To deny this reality of the church has serious consequences for sacramentology. Rahner emphasizes that the church is able to be the fundamental-sacramental sign of grace only by means of the church's humanness. [5] And this humanness is rightly able to be studied by sociologists of religion. For the humanness and (in a church of sinners) the inhumanness of the church does and will always exist.

What Rahner proposes, therefore, is that a theologian, and not only a sociologist of religion, focus specifically upon the humanness of the church. The same data and sociological principles can be used by a theologian "to arrive at a far more variegated portrayal of the people of the church," one which reflects the people of the church "as they are" and not simply "as they ought to be." (*Lumen gentium*, states Rahner, portrays the people of the church as they ought to be.) By means of a Christian anthropology, a number of elements in ecclesiology are brought into greater relief.

First among these is what Rahner describes as a "process of individualization of the people of the church." In contrast to the people of the church of past ages, there are today an ever

---

[5] Rahner, *Structure*, p. 219. The ET can be misleading. The phrase, *als mittels dieser ihrer Menschlichkeit*, is translated "through the medium of this human factor." It might be more exact to translate mittels as "by means of." This would avoid an interpretation, inconsistent with Rahner, of the "humanness" of the church as a passive medium through which God's grace flows.

increasing number of individuals within the people of the church who recognize a legitimate distinction: on the one hand there is the collective or whole committment of faith which is represented hierarchically, and on the other hand there is the individual committment of faith and its history. A central theological truth, notes Rahner, is that "salvation always takes place at the individual level." And, therefore, "the process of individualization taking place within the people of the church" is not something which the church must regrettably accept as unfortunate. Rather, says Rahner, the church should strive to achieve this individualization as a fundamental goal of the church itself.[6] This requires, consequently, that there be dialogue between the people of the church and the hierarchy. This dialogue rests on the conviction that it is no longer satisfactory for the people of the church to be simply taught —in a totally passive way— from on high. There is a demand that, instead of responding blindly to the hierarchy, a more responsible and informed response ought to take place. Such a dialogue rests on the presupposition that one both hears the other and is heard by the other.

Another manifestation of this process of individualization can be seen in the phenomenon of religious orders and other socially constituted groups of people of the church. The church, declares Rahner, is clearly the mediatrix of salvation. And since there is a "radical difference" between the mediation of salvation and the achievement of salvation, the church must respect the freedom of the individual in her/his "inalienable responsibility" and "immediacy to God."

But the church is more than the mediatrix of salvation. The church is also the "visible community of those who genuinely believe, hope, and love." Consequently, there must develop in the church formal groups that are the "upholders" and the "social

---

[6] Rahner, *Structure*, pp. 222-223. Rahner points out, for example, that the proliferation of sects within Christianity is a result in part from a failure on the part of the church to the extent that it maintains itself as a church of the masses in which all individuals are reduced to the same level. A sect is a "socially organized protest against such a church of the masses".

manifestation" of the individual charisms that occur in the church. These charisms are not the result of institutional elements of the church, but are the result of the Spirit. And so, such formal groups are not related primarily to the official ministerial church, even though there must be a recognition given such groups by the official ministerial church. Rahner calls for the courage to give such recognition and affirmation to these formal groups. He notes particularly that those who make up these groups are not to be automatically identified with those who hold ministerial office in the church. And these groups themselves cannot be seen as identical to the officially constituted worshipping community that gathers with its official ministerial presider.

b. "Non-practicing" Catholics

A second element in ecclesiology that is brought into sharper focus through a Christian anthropology is the reality often described as that of "non-practicing" or "border-line" Catholics. Rahner is critical of anyone in the church —clergy, in particular— who regards those who do not participate regularly in Sunday Mass as not "truly" belonging to the church. "The point of primary importance here is that not every refusal to participate in the church's life ipso facto involves a loss of membership of the church."

Those baptized individuals whom Rahner describes as the weary, the indifferent, and the uninterested, continue to belong to the people of the church as long as they do not in a decidedly, clearly, and publicly tangible way declare their rejection of the Christian faith. They should not be considered the concern merely of the official ministerial church.[7] A Christian anthropo-

---

[7] Rahner, *Structure*, p. 224. Rahner cautions that the church "must not adopt an attitude of latent and unexplicitated Novatianism by acting as though ... only the 'attendants at Sunday Mass' ... really belonged to her, while the rest had to be patiently put up with as 'bad Catholics.'" Rahner goes on to stress that "so long as we divide the people of the church into those who fulfill their Sunday and Easter duties and those who do not, we are, in a strange way, deciding whether individuals shall be accounted Catholics or not, not according to whether they

logy can better enable one to recognize that individuals may be doing "all that is appropriate here and now to their particular phase of religious development." The conclusion that one reaches regarding these "non-practicing" Catholics changes considerably if one's perspective changes. Rahner suggests that it is more accurate to recognize such Christians as those "who have not yet developed the course of their Christianity to that point at which an individual achieves a positive relationship to the church and her life ..." And this approach is founded upon the fact that for every person in the church —both "practicing" and "non-practicing"— "faith inevitably has an individual history and development of its own."[8] Because it is both possible and necessary to distinguish between the "committment of faith of the church as a whole" and the individual committment of faith of the individual, the result is a multitude of ways in which groups are formed within the people of the church.

One particularly strong conviction on the part of Rahner concerns the fact that the church is a sinful church of sinners. It is therefore conceivable that there may be opposing structures within the people of the church. Consequently, Rahner declares that "there must be individuals and groups within the church who are the representatives of a protest against the sinfulness and latent unbelief in the church, and the church on her side must maintain sufficient scope within herself for 'non-conformists' and 'protestants' in this sense." Rahner emphasizes that the "official representatives of the church's teaching and pastoral work" cannot in principle be excluded from such a protest. The official

---

fulfill a divine commandment but according to whether they fulfill a precept of the juris ecclesiastici" (p. 225).

[8] Rahner, *Structure*, p. 226. Rahner notes, by example, that there are groups within the people of the church in whose religious life devotion to Mary and indulgences are significant, and other groups where this is hardly the case. More noteworthy is the fact that there are on the one hand Christian ecclesial groups who view their Christianity as a legitimation of their social status, and on the other hand there are groups who view the message of the gospel as a critique of societal order.

ministerial church itself is capable of having a protest justifiably brought against it.

c. The Local Worshiping Community

A third element in ecclesiology that is brought into relief by Christian anthropology concerns what occurs at the level of the local worshipping community. Rahner states that the local worshipping community cannot be constituted as it ought to be simply on the basis of its community profession of faith and the ritual expression of that faith in liturgy. This truth, believes Rahner, was not always reflected upon with the same explicitness as today. This is due in part to the fact that in past times the structure of the parish was able to clearly presuppose an already established and integrated local social structure, particularly at the level of the village. There are two significant consequences to this fact. In the first place, the worshipping community, without an already given sociological structure, itself becomes ideological. Secondly, and one may say consequently, there is a necessity for the church to fashion the human sociological framework that will allow the local worshipping community not to remain on the level of ideology.

Some of the human factors that Rahner cites in such a framework are: the reality of being neighbors, "mutual acquaintance", and "a readiness to help one another in the secular sphere." Just as significant are the presuppositions that allow these structures to develop, for example: "a common language, similar problems to face, a level of education which is to some extent homogeneous, etc." The principle that guides Rahner in these considerations is: *gratia supponit naturam*. And he concludes that ecclesial society as such "is constituted not merely by that which belongs specifically to the church's nature (Spirit, word, sacrament, official institution [*Amt*; better translated "ministerial office"]. Rather, it presupposes and implies the 'natural' structures of an integrated society." Due to the reality of the disintegration somewhat of society today, the church has a formidable task.

Thus, in all of this, if the church is to achieve an accurate picture of the actual structures of the people of the church and respond positively to its task, it must draw upon the studies and indications that sociology can offer.

2. The Charismatic Element in the Church

a. A Theological Perspective

In an article first published in 1969 dealing with the charismatic element in the church, Rahner concludes that "the charismatic element belongs no less necessarily and abidingly to the nature of the church than her official institutions (*Amt*; more exactly translated: "ministerial office") and the sacraments."[9] His conclusion is consistent with his earlier considerations on the theme of the charismatic element in the church. He specifically notes that "no comprehensive work on this subject has yet been written."

He emphasizes that a recognition that the Spirit and grace are constitutive of the church stands in opposition to an ecclesiological Nestorianism. And of particular note is Rahner's affirmation that "in a Catholic ecclesiology we find neither in practice nor in the linguistic usage of the New Testament any opposition or hostility between the official institutions of the church (*kirchlichen Amt*; more exactly translated: "ecclesial ministerial office") on the one hand, and the charismatic element on the other." He adds that in the wake of Montanism, an often repeated attitude has been to view the charismatic element as limited to the "initial stages of the church's life."

In more recent times, the fact that the charismatic element belongs to the nature of the church itself has been affirmed in an explicit doctrinal way. Rahner notes that the terms *charisma* and *charismaticus* occur in fourteen passages of the documents of

---

[9] Rahner, *Observations on the Factor of the Charismatic in the Church* (hereafter *Charismatic Observations*) in *TI*, Vol. 12, London, 1974, pp. 81-97, esp. p. 84.

Vatican II. Nevertheless, he contends that —as is very clearly exemplfied in *Lumen gentium*— "officialdom (*Amtskirche*; more exactly translated: "the official ministerial church") still continues constantly to occupy the center of the ecclesiological stage." Rahner suggests an ecclesiology is needed that recognizes the unique character of the charismatic element. Such an ecclesiology would "regard the church primarily as the historical concretization of the charismatic as brought about by the Spirit of Christ," and would "regard the specifically institutional element in her simply as one of the regulating factors (albeit a necessary one) for this charismatic element." [10] The significant conclusion that Rahner reaches is that ministerial office (*Amt*) in the church has a charismatic character, for "gifts of the Spirit can only be regulated by a gift of the Spirit."

While charisms thus are bestowed upon those who hold ministerial office in the church, there are also non-institutional charisms. This results from the fact that the church as holy is constituted not simply of those who hold ministerial office, but that the church is the "holy people of God".

The question then arises, how does the charismatic element in the holy people of God contrast with the Christian virtues. Rahner's response is that the only difference is that in Christian virtues charisms stress or emphasize distinctive marks of the church: the social reality of the church, the characteristics of revelation, of the profession of faith, of bearing witness or carrying out the mission of the church. Since, therefore, charisms have what may be described as an ecclesial character, charisms also have a significance with regard to the world, that is, with regard to all that is non-ecclesial, since the church is the "sacrament of the world." It is specifically through these charisms that the church serves the world in the fulfillment of the church's world tasks.

---

[10] Rahner, *Charismatic Observations*, pp. 85-86. See, also, Rahner, *Courage for an Ecclesial Christianity* (hereafter *Courage*) in *TI*, Vol. 20, London, 1981, pp. 3-12.

Even though charisms are realized by the Holy Spirit, Rahner stresses that it is quite possible for the offical ministerial church to suppress charisms. This does not contradict the truth that the official ministerial church as a whole can never be opposed to the work of the Spirit as a whole. It is simply pointing out that in particular cases, even extremely important ones, those holding ministerial office in the church can act "erroneously or culpably" in suppressing or condemning what has been the result of the work of the Spirit. In a positive way, the official ministerial church has a responsibility to see that legitimate charismatic developments in the church be given the institutional embodiment that is justly sought. This should be done as soon as possible so that the work of the Spirit will be effective and continue to be effective, and that this work of the Spirit will be integrated into the life of the whole church.

b. A Sociological Perspective

As noted earlier, Rahner's ecclesiological writings in the period after Vatican II bring into clearer focus his convictions regarding the anthropological dimension of the church. This is exemplified remarkably in his reflection on the charismatic element in the church. After presenting some considerations on this theme from a theological perspective, he takes up the same theme from a more sociological perspective.

The thesis that Rahner puts forward is: "the charismatic element in the church designates that point in the church at which God as Lord of the church presides over the church as an open system." The meaning of open system is crucial. The church as an open system is "a system such that the definitive condition in which it actually stands and should stand neither can nor should be defined in any adequate sense in terms of any one point immanent within the system itself." For Rahner, God is the point which defines the reality of the church and God stands fully outside the reality of the church. The conclusion which Rahner is led to is that the respective state of this open system must be rightly produced and known as charismatic and not as institutional.[11]

Rahner sees the element of the charismatic in the church as the first and most characteristic among the formal elements of the church. Consequently, to view the charismatic and the institutional as existing merely in a dialectical relationship, with each representing the respective poles of a spectrum on an identical plane, would be to deny that the church is a fundamentally open system.

There is a difficulty that hinders or prevents the church from being recognized as an open system. In the church there is a dimension, namely that of the church's ministerial office and its juridical reality, within which there is a highest peak of authority which is not determined by any other point in this same dimension. In the Catholic church, the pope and the collective episcopate are the holders of this highest authority.[12]

Without denying this reality Rahner stresses that it is of the utmost importance to affirm that "this whole juridical dimension, taken strictly as such, is only one of the elements in the social reality of the church herself." Furthermore, this juridical dimension cannot "dominate over the total reality and the total functioning of the other elements even at the merely social level." Rahner accepts that at the juridical level there is no other inner-church authority that stands over the personal supremacy of the pope, that the pope "is not judged by anyone else." This often gives way to a misunderstanding that the pope acts "merely on his own initiative, merely as autonomous, and not accepting the ideas of others," with the consequent impression that "Peter is

---

[11] Rahner, *Charismatic Observations*, p. 89. The "state" (Zustand) of the system is achieved charismatically; and because of this, it is accurate to describe its "operations" as charismatic.

[12] Rahner, *Charismatic Observations*, p. 90. Rahner describes this authority as being "monarchical-collegial." On this theme, he refers in n. 17 to, among others, Rahner, J. Ratzinger, *The Episcopate and the Primacy* (*QD*, 4) (hereafter *Episcopate*) Freiburg, 1962, pp. 11-36. A second previously unpublished article by Rahner in *Episcopate* is entitled *On the Divine Right of the Episcopate*, pp. 64-135.)

the church, and that the church is adequately contained, reformed
and determined in its activities in Peter." To counteract this
misunderstanding, to prevent, as much as possible, this false
impression, Rahner underscores his conviction that the church
must be affirmed as an open and charismatic system.

An observable fact of church life which helps to affirm that the
church is an open system is the reality of pluralism.[13] This is
clearly emphasized in the church's teaching regarding the office of
the bishop: bishops rule their flocks "not in the name of the pope
but in the name of Christ, and hence are not mere officials of the
pope."[14] Rahner stresses the necessary conclusion that here,
"even at the juridical level, a certain inalienable pluralism is
recognized, so that ... the authority accorded to the pope is not a
totalitarian one." Another example of pluralism is the teaching
about the necessary reception of a new law by the people of the
church. A further example of the reality of pluralism is that even
the teaching office of the church can only carry out its work
"with the help of theology and of religious awareness in general
(better translated: "a general spiritual awareness"), neither of
which are simply dependent upon those official institutions."
Thus it is completely inaccurate to describe the pope as the
"pilot" who is guiding the history of the church. He is, rather,
one who is himself guided by a history to which the true pilot

[13] Rahner, *Charismatic Observations*, p. 91. "What we de facto observe in the
church throughout her entire history is a genuine pluralism within which the
papacy has a position of its own without thereby being able to determine or to
initiate the whole of that activity." An example of some of the many things that
have developed "without any influence —at any rate any notable influence— on
the part of the pope," Rahner cites: 1) the first councils; 2) almost the whole
history of dogma; 3) the origins of religious orders; 4) the greater part of the
history of spirituality; 5) the life of the churches of the Far East; 6) and the history
of theology.

[14] Rahner, *Charismatic Observations*, p. 91. Rahner states that the office of
bishop is *juris divini*. He emphasizes this as a reality by stressing that a bishop rules
"in the name of Christ" and not "in the name of the pope." This comparison
needs to be kept in mind as Rahner's fundamental point. It would be a gratuitous
interpretation to describe "in the name of the pope" as synonomous with "in the
name of the church." Rather, the bishop rules in the name of the church, and thus
in the name of Christ.

does not belong. This expresses an essential element of what the church is as an open system: the church as "the exodus, the people on pilgrimage toward the inconceivable mystery of God."

In all of this, Rahner concludes that the word charismatic is a key term "to stand for that ultimate incalculability which belongs to all the other elements in the church in their mutual interplay." In this sense Rahner agrees that the charismatic element in the church can and should be seen as "transcendental in character." At the same time, this charismatic element also is seen as something that is concrete and categorical which is expressed by the innerworldly openness of history as creative freedom. This very concrete element of historical freedom would be that which is charismatic in the church. Through the grace of the Spirit this openness to an innerworldly future becomes, for the members of the church, a mediation of an openness to an absolute future.

c. Obedience in an "Open System"

A "third question" which Rahner focuses upon in regard to the charismatic element in the church is formulated as a question concerning ecclesiastical obedience. His main point is that at the concrete level of church life it is inevitable in an open system that there is and will be conflict experienced between "charismatic prophets" who have a consciousness of their mission and the official ministerial church with its leadership. Obedience in a closed system is such that "authority decides everything and is itself influenced by no one." But the nature of obedience in an open system is an obedience such that "each party influences the other, ... an obedience which allows for personal initiative."[15] The task in an open system is an ongoing, ever-renewed responsiblity for each person to work out a synthesis between the responsible taking of initiative on the one hand and obedience on the other."[16]

---

[15] Rahner, *Charismatic Observations*, p. 95. Such an obedience must allow for the possibility that an individual may determine that s/he is called in conscience not to carry out a particular directive.

[16] Rahner, *Charismatic Observations*, p. 97. Rahner makes the emphatic point

Ultimately, obedience must appeal to the free initiative and the individual responsible decision of the one responding in the church. Therefore, the church —recognizing that the institutional element in the church is legitimate— remains encompassed by the workings of the Spirit in the church. It is the Spirit which leads the open system of the church ever again towards a future which cannot be planned ahead adequately by individuals or the institution. It is a future which the Spirit, and no one else, has decreed.

3. Structural Change in the Church

The theme of structural change in the church is a theme which is closely related to Rahner's reflections on the charismatic element in the church. In fact, for Rahner the charismatic element in the church provides the framework for structural change in the church. Significantly Rahner has devoted particular interest to the theme of structural change in the church.

a. Structural Change and Sacramentology

From a pastoral point of view, Rahner raises the question as to why there is often so much conflict and tension in the church regarding structural change. He particularly notes an acute anta-

---

that a "solution" cannot be arrived at by giving final preference to the institution: "It might be suggested that we should content ourselves with a statement that in cases of conflict between the official institutions (Amt; more exactly: 'ministerial office') and the charismatic elements, it is the official institutions that have the last word (although not the penultimate one), so that our obedience is due to them. The validity of this can indeed be admitted as a certain practical rule of thumb. But the problem is not solved thereby. For the only 'last word' in the true sense is concerned with what has already taken place or is brought into being by this word. So far as the future is concerned there is no 'last word' in the proper sense. For even one who actually obeys a directive can still always take into account that at a later stage such a directive will be withdrawn, that the situation will change radically and will thus render the controversial directive superfluous, that as generation succeeds to generation in the church, as theology progresses, etc., many directives are rendered out of date, and thus a whole new-scope for the charismata is created in the church" (pp. 96-97).

gonism between conservative and progressive tendencies in the church. [17] His response is that in secular societies structural change is concerned fundamentally with matters that are of relative importance. In the church, structural change is also concerned with matters that are of relative importance, that is, inner-worldly and human realities, but precisely these realities are seen to be related "sacramentally" to the "divine sphere," to human beings' eternal destiny and salvation.

These realities take on an importance that goes beyond purely secular realities. Realities such as the word of scripture and actual sacramental signs are mediations of the relationship of the believer to that which is eternal. And so if a believer has the impression that ordinary church realities mediate really and in a vital way her/his relationship to God and her/his salvation, or, on the contrary, that such church realities are hindering or blocking her/his relationship to God and salvation, this individual is going to be committed to maintaining what works and changing what does not. The intensity of the struggle that can and does occur in the church concerning earthly realities results from the fact that the earthly and the eternal "cannot very easily be clearly distinguished either objectively or emotionally."

The "solution" that Rahner suggests is that both those with a conservative tendency and those with a progressive tendency not conclude that their own position is absolute. In effect, "conservatives and progressives can prematurely and by over-simplication associate or even identify what is relative and historically conditioned with what is eternal and perennially valid." Rahner's implicit basic principle regarding sacramentology, which is radically christological, is that the human and divine are affirmed as inseparable and also unconfused.

---

[17] Rahner, *Structural Change in the Church of the Future* (hereafter *Change*) in *TI*, Vol. 20; London, 1981, pp. 115-132, esp. pp. 130-132.

b. Structural Change and Ius Divinum

1° An Historical Shift from "Unchangeability"

The "Pian era" of the church delineates, for Rahner, the period following the French Revolution up to the Second Vatican Council. He states that a dominant description of the church during this period is that of its unchangeability. Two historical factors influenced the church's self-understanding in this period: 1) the church ceased to be one with a homogenous Christian society, and consequently felt threatened, defensive, scorned (e.g., through anti-clericalism), and thus in need of relying more or less exclusively on itself; 2) the reality of history itself was not incorporated in any significant way into medieval and baroque theology —history was viewed as all that is contingent, history was not seen as "the history of essences and of the transcendence of human beings to God."[18]

A significant shift has taken place since Vatican II regarding the church's self-understanding. The possiblity of change in the structure of the church is seen to be much greater than was the case in the Pian era.

Rahner's thesis regarding change in the church of its "creed, life, and juridical constitution" is significant. "In the concrete it is not so simple to decide where the distinction is to be drawn between changeable and unchangeable factors in the church." These are not simply seen as two entities "existing side by side as immediately empirically apprehensible each in its own right."[19]

---

[18] Rahner, *Change*, pp. 117-118. The "a priori unhistorical" orientation of medieval and baroque theology was preserved and revived in neoscholasticism. In a scholastic Denziger-theology, for example, authentic statements of the magisterium were treated in practice as if they had the binding force of dogma and measures passed by curial officials regarded almost as straightforward decisions of the pope using his supreme power of jurisdiction (p. 118).

[19] Rahner, *Basic Observations on the subject of Changeable and Unchangeable Factors in the Church* (hereafter *Changeable and Unchangeable*), in *TI*, vol. 14, London, 1976, pp. 3-23. The approach that Rahner is struggling against is one which —explicitly or otherwise— gives the impression that it is possible to arrive at that which is unchangeable with an "absolute certainty." Rahner denies this. That which is unchangeable is not ultimately able to be experienced in any "pure" form.

Rather, it is the factor of change which is "more immediate" and "more apprehensible." And he insists that it is precisely in the changeable —that is, "that which we immediately experience and make living contact with"— that "this unchangeable factor has ever afresh to be believed in, hoped in, and acted upon in a spirit of faithfulness as that which is the more hidden of the two factors." The conclusion for Rahner is that only in and through the experience of change can one truly realize her/his fidelity towards that which is unchangeable. So, being "on the way to a goal, ... being on pilgrimage" is a primary characteristic of the individual Christian who seeks that which is unchangeable.

At the same time, while affirming that the unchangeable is always found in the changeable, that is, that the two are inseparable, Rahner is equally insistent that the changeable and unchangeable remain unconfused with respect to each other. It is precisely here that Rahner criticizes the "traditional neo-scholastic theology," one which Rome seems to depend upon exclusively, as a theology that "has failed to see that many questions are still open questions. ... The failure to recognize these open questions leads all too easily to a narrow interpretation of these dogmas that do require assent. ... Open questions and dogma are mixed together."[20]

2° The Roman See

The changeable and unchangeable factors in the church's own structure are a principle interest in this book, particularly with

[20] See the extremely significant article, Rahner, *Open Questions in Dogma Considered by the Institutional Church as Definitively Answered* (hereafter *Open Questions*) in *Journal of Ecumenical Studies* (hereafter *JES*) 15 (1978) 211-226. See, also, Rahner, *FCF*, pp. 391-398, in which Rahner deals with the necessary law and order in the church, and with the "levels of relativity in the law." A conclusion that he reaches is that "the imposition of laws in the church is a real self-actualization of the church as a society (*Gesellschaft*) and as a pneumatic community (*Gemeinschaft*) only if the law is maintained with a humility and a spirit of service which knows that law in God's church can provide space for his life and his grace, and even provide their presence. But nevertheless and for this reason it may not simply be identified with God and his Spirit and with what is supposed to be mediated by this law" (p. 398).

regard to those elements "which are beyond dispute so far as Catholic ecclesiology is concerned, namely (1) the primatial power of the pope and (2) the episcopal structure of the Roman Catholic church."[21]

Rahner notes that for many today there is a recognition that "the supreme and permanent power of jurisdiction of the pope for the whole church is not simply identical with the whole gigantic administrative machinery which has developed historically."[22] More fundamentally, the "primatial power of the pope is also restricted and by human law can impose on itself limits required by a particular historical situation."[23] One important restriction, and one which Rahner declares cannot simply be taken for granted, is that "canonically unlimited primacy" is limited by "Christian moral norms, including some that are not always the same materially, but vary according to the historical situation."[24]

In regard to restrictions that have been self-imposed by the papacy, Rahner points to the reality of concordats. In these cases, the Holy See has voluntarily restricted its (legitimate) jurisdiction

---

[21] Rahner, *Changeable and Unchangeable*, pp. 17-23, esp. p. 17. Rahner also considers the theme of unchangeable dogma, pp. 8-14; and the theme of an unchangeable ethic, pp. 14-16.

[22] Rahner, *Change*, p. 119. "The demarcation between what the pope admits and up to a point must admit to belong to the autonomous competence of the particular church and what he reserves to himself for the most part is not a matter of divine law, but has come to existence historically and is therefore changeable."

[23] Rahner, *Change*, p. 120. Divine law, notes Rahner, certainly restricts papal power. For example, the pope "cannot abolish the episcopate" nor "replace it by office-holders who would merely be his officials". See, also, Rahner, *Open Questions*, p. 219, where, Rahner reiterates that bishops cannot become simply "regional representatives of the pope." And he adds: "this danger has not yet been eliminated even today."

[24] Rahner, *Open Questions*, pp. 219-220. Rahner does not dispute the fact that in general the pope respects and recognizes the limits imposed by Christian moral norms. "But ... it is quite conceivable that certain moral limitations which derive necessarily from a modern social and cultural situation are objectively present but not recognized and therefore not respected. For example, it is in principle quite conceivable that Pope Paul VI by the publication of the encyclical *Humanae vitae*, though in good faith, still offended in practice norms governing the pope's reaching a judgment".

so as to obtain a more favorable situation for the church in a particular country. The conclusion that Rahner underscores is that "if this sort of thing is possible in relations between church and State, it can be possible also in relations between the Roman See and other authorities and groups within the church." Nevertheless, these self-imposed restrictions by the Holy See must truly be self-imposed. Rahner is very clear that "for the sake of unity and peace in the church the pope must be granted the competence to decide his own competence."

Rahner indicates some examples of how the Roman See can restrict itself in order to allow a greater flexibility on the level of the particular churches. One example is particularly noteworthy. He states that it is not necessary that Rome must determine for the whole church the norms for the selection of priests. These norms, such as the law of celibacy, the exclusion of women from the priesthood, and determining the sacramental levels of the one ministerial office are norms that could be determined by a particular church. Rahner is principally arguing that the Roman See not block the possibilities that can legitimately allow particular churches to bring about changes in the structure of the church.[25] One element in the significance of his argument is that structural change in the church is more likely to come about "from below" rather than "from above." But, whatever changes occur need to be "structured" changes, ones that are incorporated into the life of the church. Frequently it is the particular church that can more readily respond to this need.

---

[25] Rahner, *Change*, pp. 121-122. See, also, *Open Questions*, pp. 218-223, in which Rahner treats the same theme from an ecumenical perspective: "There can be no doubt whatsoever that much of what is claimed by the Roman See as historically-acquired powers and rights of the Roman See do not in fact pertain dogmatically to the inalienable essence of the primacy... Rome should state clearly what does not pertain to the essence of the primacy and what it is prepared to renounce in dealing with churches that seek union with Rome" (219). In regard to celibacy, Rahner states: "For me it is not self-evident and obvious that the regulation about sacerdotal celibacy should be unilaterally determined for the church (in der ganzen Kirche!) by Rome" (220).

3° Episcopal "Democratic" Structures in the Church

The episcopal structure of the church, like the primatial power of the pope, is an unchanging element of the structure of the church. Yet today this unchanging element can itself become much more "democratic" as a structure of the church. Rahner envisions this particularly with respect to diocesan churches and national churches. [26]

What is important to affirm is that the people of the church have the necessity of participating and collaborating in the life of the church and in the decisions of the ministerial office. This is a necessity because the people of the church are not simply receivers of the product produced by the offical ministerial church; the people of the church are the church. The crucial point, according to Rahner, is that today the real efficacy of the ministerial office in the church —that is, proclamation of the Gospel, celebration of the sacraments, leadership, and so forth— depends to a great extent on the free cooperation of the people of the church. And the people of the church are not going to freely cooperate unless they share to the greatest extent possible in the decision-making processes of the official ministerial church.

Thus, seen in terms of sacramentology, Rahner argues that the involvement of the people of the church is a necessary condition if ministerial office in the church is to achieve its full sacramental efficacy. Because Rahner judges this participation to be essential, he sees it as necessary to fashion appropriate juridical and clear structures. Something so essential should not depend exclusively upon the good will of whoever may be exercising ministerial office in the church.

As to the extent that the participation of the people of the church is to be seen as being a deliberative, and not merely a consultative voice, this is a question that needs to be addressed honestly and courageously. An adequate answer can only be given in response to concrete particular cases.

---

[26] Rahner, *Change*, pp. 122-125. "national churches" (*nationale Kirchen*) should be distinguished from the term *Volkskirche* which Rahner uses to describe culturally and socially homogeneous "popular" churches.

Another question that deserves serious study, declares Rahner, is whether it is part of the divine law (ius divinum) that the episcopal power, a necessary power in the church, must be exercised exclusively by an individual. Does the structure of the monarchic episcopate "exclude a synodal or presbyteral structure of the church *iure divino* even if the authority of a bishop as understood in the Catholic sense were to be ascribed to a small collegiate body of this kind?"[27]

Underlying Rahner's question is his premise that it is not possible to encounter an "abiding divine law" in itself. "The *ius divinum* of the church always and wherever it exists has a concreteness which is not itself *iuris divini* ... What we find ourselves directly confronted with in the constitutional law of the church either to our joy or to our sorrow is the changeable element." The changeable element mediates that which is unchangeable. Rahner conceives of the changeable and unchangeable in sacramental terms: "it is precisely and solely in this (the changeable) that the abiding nature of this constitutional law as given to the church by God can become present and effective."

In order to avoid, on the one hand, a "false conservatism" which proclaims "a state of absolute unchangeableness in the church in all matters" and, on the other hand, a view that espouses that change in the church proceeds in a completely arbitrary way, Rahner stresses the absolutely necessary committment to discern what is the changeable and what is the unchangeable. He specifically speaks of this in terms of a discernemnt of spirits. It is a task to which the church must dedicate itself to the best of its ability.

In addition to a committment to a "discernment of spirits" with respect to the changeable and the unchangeable, Rahner emphasizes another important factor: the courage to experiment. This is a necessity because Rahner notes that the difference

---

[27] Rahner, *Changeable and Unchangeable*, pp. 19-20. Rahner's own opinion: "I believe that nowadays in Catholic theology we can still leave the question open as to whether the possibility of episcopal power being vested in a collegiate or presbyteral body is really irreconcilable with the principle of episcopal constitution."

between the changeable and unchangeable in the church cannot in many cases be discerned by means of theoretical reason. "A process of experimentation is precisely the manner in which the discernment of spirits is achieved by the practical reason."[28]

c. Structural Change: The Postulate of Tutiorism

Rahner calls on the church to develop a strategy based on the postulate of tutiorism. Tutiorism is not at all a justification for a "timid conservatism." For he says "in the long run, the safest course and the one that will do the least harm is to muster the courage now to attempt what in all probability will be demanded of the institutional church tomorrow."[29] Tutiorism of change, for Rahner, expresses a mentality in the church in which risk and experimentation can and must "creatively and courageously inaugurate many structural changes in the church." This risk and experimentation is judged to be, under the circumstances, the "safest" and, at the same time, the "necessary" course of action.

Rahner invokes this bold postulate of tutiorism because he is convinced that the church must experience structural change or it will not be the effective sacrament of salvation of the world that it is meant to be. The structural change that is necessary is such that will make the church more one than it has been. Today, this requirement that the church be more one is manifested in two particular ways: a) the shifting of the church from a "popular" church to a community church; b) the task of ecumenism.

1° Community Church: Declericalized, Serving, Caring

The church needs to recognize that it can no longer see itself primarily as a "popular" church. Paradoxically, this means that the church is at the same time a diaspora-church and a world-church. It is found almost everywhere in the world, but not as a "popular" church as in the past. Consequently, the church cannot rely so much upon the sociological conditions that have formed

---

[28] Rahner, *Changeable and Unchangeable*, pp. 22-23.
[29] Rahner, *Change*, p. 130; "institutional church" = *Amtskirche*.

the framework of the church as a "popular" church. These conditions are waning. Rather, the church needs to be supported by a framework of basic communities, which are formed through the free faith-decisions of individuals.

All of these factors indicate to Rahner that the church must be able to be conceived of, described, and experienced as a "declericalized, serving, caring church." This is the reality that structural change must reflect and strive for in the church. It must be a declericalized church because the real efficacy of the church and of those who hold ministerial office depends on the free, personal faith committment of members of the church and their consequent participation in the actual life of the church. This can be achieved in part by: 1) "a greater 'democratization' ... of the church, not restricting the collaborations of the 'laity' to purely consultative functions...; 2) greater openness in decision-making in the church's life, specifically for the non-clerical member of the church."

2° Ecumenism: Structural Changes as Necessary Conditions

With respect to ecumenism, structural change in the church should take place wherever this is possible. Structural changes today can allow the separated Christian churches to see more clearly that they belong together, and that they can more easily be in agreement, working for the goal of being united in the one true unity of the one church of Christ.

Rahner suggests that the large particular churches, such as those in Africa, Asia, and Latin America, must be given entirely new room for the realization of what is uniquely their own. In accepting and affirming the reality of the church as a world-church, Rahner questions whether the law of the world-church can be as "Roman" as it has been. Specifically in regard to ecumenism, he states that the entire question of a reciprocal recognition of ministerial office has to be addressed with much more "theological energy and confidence." With more theological creativity and less fear, he believes, a solution that is both ambitious and possible can be achieved.

The Catholic church should recognize that structural changes are necessary as conditions for allowing a Christianity that is one to be achieved. If the Catholic Church does not realize these structural changes, the church, as separated, will not be able to fulfill its task in the world as fully as it should. The basic principle for Rahner is that the church, living in society, "must develop its concrete structures in dialogue and confrontation, in order to secure as well as possible its endurance, its life and its missionary activity in that future society."

4. Relationship of Church and World

Two years after Rahner's essay on church and World was published as an article in *Sacramentum Mundi*, he offered further considerations on this theme. His starting point for these particular reflections has a pastoral dimension. His thesis refers to the salvation-task of the church, asking the question as to whether "this task of the church as such is concerned with the humanization of the world and nothing beyond this." He notes that such an approach has been labeled "pure horizontalism."

a. Pure Horizontalism

Rahner identifies three particular reasons behind the emergence of this horizontalism: 1) "the tendency towards demythologization"; 2) "the rationalism of the natural sciences"; and 3) the active change of human beings and the human environment by human beings themselves. In effect, horizontalism seeks to reinterpret —or simply interpret— the salvific task of the church from a context relating to these three factors.

b. Unity of Love of God and Love of Neighbor

In response, Rahner argues against an approach that would simply counter with a need for a verticalism as the "other" necessary dimension of Christianity. This is not a satisfactory solution. Rather, Rahner is quick to emphasize that the experience of the world is that which mediates an experience of God. "There is no experience of God for the pilgrim human being on this earth which has not been mediated through an experience of the world." He goes on to point out that even the immediacy of the relationship between God and human beings which is the result of God's graced self-communication "is always mediated through the experience of the world which human beings find already about them."[30]

The relationship of the individual and of the church as such to the world is fundamentally and principally a relationship not to the material environment but to the human environment. Only through this relationship can a human being realize her/himself as a subject who is capable of "transcendent experiences of freedom, responsibility, absolute truth, love and personal trust." It is through this human I-Thou experience that the human being is enabled to understand God, not as a part of the world of objects, but as the "ground, the horizon and the ultimate goal" of the personal horizontal movement of the human being to her/his human environment.

Through this experience the human being is consequently able to experience God as a personal direct partner in a relationship that is unmediated, a relationship that is freely initiated and realized by God. Fundamentally, "there is a mutually conditioning relationship between our relationship to our neighbor and our relationship to that which we call God." It is essential, therefore, to affirm the unity between love of neighbor and love of God, and thus between horizontalism and verticalism. There is an "indissoluble unity in the midst of distinction".

Rahner notes that in one way there is a priority of the vertical over the horizontal, and in another way a priority of the horizontal

---

[30] Rahner, *The Church's Commission to Bring Salvation and in Humanization of the World*, in *TI*, Vol. 14, London, 1974, p. 304. It is this experience of grace that enables a human being, as a child of God, to call God Father. See, also, Rahner, *Theological Justification of the Church's Development Work* (hereafter *Development*) in *TI*, Vol. 20, London, 1981, pp. 65-73.

over the vertical. But in both cases, one must never forget that the two are "absolutely mutually conditioning" the one to the other. There are times and circumstances, insists Rahner, when that which is most urgent and most demanded is not necessarily that which is "objectively speaking the most important and the most valuable." In this light he declares that the church can "emphasize the duty of love of neighbor more radically than she has done in earlier ages, because the Christian's responsibility for the world now includes quite fresh tasks and duties such as simply did not exist in former times." At the same time the church cannot abandon "for a couple of decades" its worship, its theology, its "cultivation of an interior religious orientation to God" while dedicating itself wholeheartedly to a love of neighbor.

c. Conclusions

Rahner draws some important conclusions. He states that the church as the official ministerial church "is not the immediate or proper subject for realizing in the concrete the humanization of the world." If the church were to assume this position, the result would be a clericalism or sacralism. This would be a failure on the part of the church to recognize and respect the legitimate autonomy of the world which is not subject "to the direct guidance of the official church". Yet, paradoxically, the church, by declaring itself not competent to be the subject of the humanization of the world, is able, both through its ministerial office, as well as through other members of the church, to offer a critique of the sociological conditions that require change.

More significant is the fact that by not seeking to be the subject of the humanization of the world, the church can carry out its own "true saving task which she alone can fulfill." What is this task of the church? It is to announce "that it is only through God's grace that we are set free in such a way as to be able to use and enjoy the world, and open ourselves unreservedly to our neighbor without being enslaved by this social and material environment, without having to idolize it." But even more, this grace of God must, in a bodily sign, be offered and communicated to the world. And the historical, bodily self-communication of God in the death and resurrection of Jesus Christ must be continually accepted and celebrated anew "precisely because this self-utterance of God takes place in the world as such. All this is included in the salvific task of the church."

This emphatic conclusion by Rahner in regard to the relationship between church and world leads me to consider in more depth an important theme in Rahner's ecclesiology: the church as the sacrament of the salvation of the world. This is a theme of his ecclesiology that is directly linked to his reflections on the relationship of church and world. For, in focusing upon the central importance of love of neighbor, Rahner declares: "the other person, who is loved, is the sacrament in whom we receive God."[31]

5. Church: Basic Sacrament of Salvation

a. Origin (Herkunft) of the Church

In a 1976 lecture dealing with the question of the institution of the church by Jesus, Rahner remarks that he is first of all a systematic theologian. While he does not claim to be an exegete as such, he does wish to recognize certain important conclusions that have been reached through the historical sciences about this question of the origin of the church. Put simply, the question is this: "Can we speak of an institution of the church by Jesus?"

Rahner identifies two distinct ecclesiologies: 1) the sociological ecclesiology of fundamental theology;[32] and 2) the properly soteriological dogmatic ecclesiology.[33] The difficulty that he

[31] Rahner, *Development*, p. 71. See, also, Rahner, *FCF*, pp. 398-400, a section entitled: *The Church as the place for love of God and of neighbor*.

[32] Rahner, *The Church's Redemptive Historical Provenance for the Death and Resurrection of Jesus*, in *TI*, Vol. 19, London, 1984, p. 26. "This ecclesiology is concerned in terms of the institution of a specific society" (p. 25).

[33] Rahner, *Church's Provenance*, p. 26. The Pauline description of the church

notes is that these two ecclesiologies have not been adequately reconciled with each other. More serious yet is that today the institution of the society of the church is able to be linked with Jesus only with great difficulty.

One theological question that poses a problem to this sociological ecclesiology is that of the expectation of Jesus' imminent return. A second question is the recognition of a great deal of diversity specifically within the New Testament period with regard to church structure.[34]

The fundamental question Rahner seeks to resolve is how one can legitimately maintain that Jesus instituted the church and at the same time accept the basic conclusions that have been reached by historical-critical biblical scholarship.

His position is to present a much broader and richer interpretation of the concept of institution. He notes that generally the terminology of institution is seen as synonymous with the concept of a verbal, juridical organization of a society. The concept of institution does not, however, need to be understood in such a narrow way. His thesis is this: "The church comes from the death and resurrection of Jesus as part of the eschatological perma-

as the mystical body of Christ exemplifies, declares Rahner, this type of ecclesiology.

[34] Rahner, *Church's Provenance*, p. 27. "The church in the New Testament times in Judaistic and Hellenistic areas or elsewhere does not present the image of something absolutely fully constructed as it is described in traditional ecclesiology as the institution of Jesus." See, also, Rahner, *FCF*, pp. 335-342, where Rahner presents an overview of the church in the New Testament and his conclusions regarding unity and variety in the New Testament image of church: "We see just from this brief sketch that the New Testament image of the church has very many levels. We find a church which is clearly institutional. It has bishops, deacons and presbyters, and is organized —particular offices and powers have a definite rank and place in the church. The individual communities are somehow connected organizationally. On the other hand we also have a theology of the church which looks especially to the interior reality of the church in grace and in faith, for example, when it is seen as the pilgrim people of God, as the community of those who are gathered around Christ as witnesses, as the body of Christ into which an individual is incorporated by baptism, the body of Christ which is quickened and constituted ever anew by the celebration of the Lord's Supper. In spite of the many images in these developing views, ultimately there does exist a deeper unity in the idea of the church in the New Testament" (p. 340).

nence of the Crucified and Risen One." For Rahner, the concept of "coming forth from" interprets —but does not replace— the concept of the "institution" of the church by Jesus.

b. Church: Basic Sacrament (Grundsakrament)

The central point of Rahner's thesis is rooted in his Christology: "through the death and resurrection of Jesus this actually ambivalent salvation history in acceptance or rejection of God's self-offering does in fact have a definitively good outcome." It has this victorious outcome because Jesus is one with God and one with human beings. God's grace is fully accepted by Jesus in a definitive and final way through his death and resurrection. The death of Jesus manifests definitively his humanity —his solidarity and oneness with all human beings. His resurrection manifests his divinity —his solidarity and oneness with God.

Since it is precisely the full acceptance of God's grace that occurs uniquely in Jesus, it is necessary that Jesus' presence remain permanently in the world, if the outcome is truly a victorious outcome for humanity. Jesus "is what he is only if this community of faith is always there in the world, to make sure that he remains historically as God's eschatological promise to the world."[35] Without this community, "Jesus does not exist at all as God's self-promise to the world." Rahner explicitly describes this community of faith, the church, as "sacrament" of the salvation of the world, as the "primordial baptism" of the world as a whole.[36] In an even more precise manner, he describes the church "as the basic sacrament of salvation" (Grundsakrament), as the "continuing presence of the eschatological salvation-act of Jesus Christ". The church, fundamentally, exists as the continua-

---

[35] Rahner, Church's Provenance, p. 32. Rahner is stressing that the church "effects," "brings about" the historical presence of Jesus. The ET fails to translate this understanding.

[36] Rahner, Church's Provenance, p. 32. Rahner notes that the church as sacrament of the salvation of the world is this regardless of its fixed size and sociological might. See, also, Rahner, Religious Feeling Inside and Outside the Church (hereafter Religious) in TI, Vol. 17, London, 1981, pp. 228-242

tion of this historical, tangible self-promise of God which is eschatological and irreversible.[37] This church, declares Rahner, is not seen so much as a "community of those who are saved, but as the sacramental primordial sign and the germ-cell of salvation for the whole world."

The church does come forth from Jesus. It is the sacrament of the salvation of the world. But the question of how this church is realized in the concrete as coming forth from Jesus and thus as the sacrament of the salvation of the world presents very serious problems. The traditional response of fundamental theology, concludes Rahner, is very difficult to support.[38]

Rahner calls for an appreciation that "history follows a single track, it is a kind of one-way street on which historically irreversible decisions are continually happening." What he underscores is that history, by necessity, commits itself to the concrete. History cannot be otherwise. For the church, an element that is unchangeable is realized in a changeable way by means of concrete, historical decisions. Each historical decision is definitive. This does not mean that the need to realize the unchangeable in the changeable comes to an end with the apostolic age —or with any subsequent age for that matter. This is, declares Rahner, an open question.

Nevertheless, the fundamental point that Rahner makes is that "we can and must regard, explain and hold on to such free decisions in apostolic times ... as wholly of divine law, without ascribing them to a verbally explicit will of Jesus to institute a

[37] Rahner, *Church's Provenance*, p. 33. See, also, Rahner's comments on the church as basic sacrament of salvation and the church as basic sacrament of salvation "for the world" in Rahner, *The Future of the Church and the Church of the Future* (hereafter *Church Future*) in *TI*, Vol. 20, London, 1981, pp. 103-114; originally given as a lecture 23 September 1977.

[38] Rahner, *Church's Provenance*, p. 33. "According to this theology, Jesus chose twelve apostles, thereby instituting the episcopate; when he took Peter from this group, he appointed the first pope." But, as Rahner indicates, Peter "seems to have played practically no part in the Pauline communities." And with regard to the episcopal constitutional structure of the church, this "first appears as explicitly developed with Ignatius of Antioch, and, in the third century, with Cyprian and others."

church." This conclusion of Rahner also has important consequences with regard to how one views the relationship of Jesus to the individual sacraments. This is of particular interest with regard to the sacramentology of ministerial office, since Rahner insists that the history of the church is and remains an "open and quite unpredictable history."

In three very relevant examples, he says that we do not know "whether the church will perhaps learn suddenly or slowly that women, too, can be holders of the priestly office." Also, we do not know whether the church slowly is learning that an academic formation of priests "is not perhaps so absolutely necessary as we imagine today." Thirdly, we do not know whether perhaps it will be much clearer that an individual who shows her/himself "from below" as a charismatic leader of a basic community will also receive sacramental approbation "from above." These and other examples help make it clear that historical developments and changes have taken place and will continue to take place in the church.

What Rahner emphasizes is that the church fundamentally testifies to the fact that God's love is successful. The church testifies to this more and more precisely as the church is sociologically organized. This church, as sociologically organized, testifies that even though the reality of sin is present, God's grace is victorious. What is fundamental, declares Rahner, is to affirm that the church really comes forth from Jesus Christ, the crucified and risen one, "despite all its [the church's] historicity and also despite all the historicity of what is called its divine constitutional laws." The church, coming forth from Jesus, the crucified and risen one, is the basic sacrament of the salvation of the world.

c. Relationship between Grundsakrament and Ursakrament

Rahner's terminology with regard to sacrament clearly manifests a development. In 1960, for example, he speaks of the church as *Ursakrament*, quickly clarifying that he sees the church as such "in relation to the single sacraments, not to Christ." In an earlier article, "Membership" (1947), his use of the term *Ursakrament* as applied to the church does not yet manifest such a nuanced approach. At this point he simply wishes to stress that the church is both "together with Christ and his grace" but also "distinguished from this grace." In this same context he speaks of the sacramental dimension of membership in the church as a *sakramentale Urzeichen* ("sacramental 'primordial' sign"). In the article, *Church of Sinners*, also from 1947, Rahner uses the term *Ursakrament* for the church, still insisting, however, on the distinction between the church as sign of grace and the church as filled with grace.

A more nuanced terminology can be seen in his 1967 article, *New Image*. But it is more than a question of refining terminology. There is a new theological emphasis. Rahner uses the term *sacramentum* in the context of the church's relationship to the world, and not primarily as descriptive of the constitutional structure of the church. One notes an equivalency in terminology in describing the church as *sacramentum* and *Grundsakrament*. Fundamental to an understanding of the church as *Grundsakrament* is first affirming the church as a diaspora church; this basic view is already presented by Rahner in "Position of Christians," (1954).

Consequently, the church is seen as the *Grundsakrament* which is a reference to the grace of God precisely where that grace is not manifested in its full ecclesial expression. The church is also *Grundsakrament* inasmuch as it is the manifestation of God as grace in its social and historical fullness. And it is in this dialectic that the terms *Ursakrament* and *Grundsakrament* particularly contrast with each other. For the pledge of salvation manifests itself above all as a primordial-sacramental pledge in Jesus Christ. And then it is the church which, as the historical continuation of Christ's existence, manifests this pledge as a fundamental-sacramental pledge.

Thus, to speak of the church as *Grundsakrament* is not simply to contrast this in a negative way with Jesus Christ, *Ursakrament*, but positively to recognize the church as the affirmation of the salvation of the world that takes place "outside" the church, in the "non-ecclesial world," in what can be described as anonymous Christianity. This relationship between church and world is dealt with explicitly by Rahner in 1968. In his article on this topic in SM he describes the church as the *Grundsakrament* which manifests that "in the unity, activity, fraternity, etc. of the world, the kingdom of God is at hand."

In 1976 Rahner focuses directly on the relationship between Jesus and the church. In a 1979 lecture, he declares that a Christian believes "that the church truly comes from Jesus Christ and consequently that it is the basic (better: 'fundamental') sacrament of salvation for the whole world". Thus, the relationship between the church and Jesus is described particularly by the term *Herkünftigkeit*. And the relationship between the church and the non-ecclesial world is described by affirming the church as *Grundsakrament*. Jesus Christ is seen as *Ursakrament* in that he is the definitive pledge of God's salvation in whom salvation is accepted, and so, realized.

PART TWO

MINISTERIAL OFFICE

THE MEANING OF
THE ONE MINISTERIAL OFFICE

The focus of Part One lays on foundational aspects of Rahner's theology and a presentation of the principle themes that emerge in Rahner's own ecclesiology. Rahner's sacramentology and ministerial office comes to the fore in Part Two. This first chapter looks specifically to Rahner's treatment of ministerial office itself and episcopal ministerial office.

1. Fundamental Starting Points

a. The Directness and Unity between God and Human Beings

Rahner does not begin his approach to the ministerial office of the church from a strictly historical perspective. Certainly he recognizes the importance of the question concerning the relationship between "the church and her concrete (more exactly: 'particular') structure as they appear on the one hand in the New Testament, especially in the pre-paschal Jesus, and on the other hand as they appear now."[1] He gives some indication of how to respond to a problem that he does not judge to be "impenetrable" (more exactly: "meaningless"). He clearly points out that the reality of history — with its ultimately insoluble details — always has a certain prerogative over analytical speculation. Nevertheless, he declares that his interest is not to focus on the construction of the church's constitutional structure — or its developmental origin — but to make an attempt to better under-

[1] Rahner, *The Meaning of Ecclesiastical Office* (hereafter *Meaning*) in Rahner, *Servants of the Lord* (hereafter *SL*), London, 1968, pp. 13-45.

stand this as it is present today. The original context of these considerations, first offered in 1966, further emphasizes this starting point on Rahner's part.

The fundamental theological position which grounds Rahner's remarks on the ministerial office of the church is that the office itself can only be understood within the context of the fact that God has united himself in a direct way with humanity, and that this unity is necessarily historically manifested. Therefore, from the beginning, it is wrong to conceive of ministerial office as something which bridges a "gulf" between God and humanity. Rather, the ministerial office of the church manifests the eschatological historicalness of this reality, and thus brings it about in very determined sacramental and word-adhering ways. Ministerial office of the church only comes about because God's unity with humanity occurs and this unity manifests itself historically.

Consequently, a fundamental thesis that emerges for Rahner is that he does not view the priesthood, for example, as a "higher degree" of being Christian. Instead he sees priesthood as a determined function — admittedly of a very imperative type — in the church, as church is affirmed as a sociological reality.   At the heart of Rahner's position is his Christology, such that he views the creation of the world from the perspective of God's self-communication — in and through Christ — to the world.

b. A Community to Bear Witness to Jesus

1° Witness to God's Victorious Love

Rahner makes an important distinction. The community of the children of God is not identical with the community which witnesses to Jesus. What he signifies by this distinction is that "by the infinite power of God's historical gift of himself those children are found everywhere, in all ages, in a countless multitude of forms, in all colors." But the reality which takes place in "the depths of world history" by God's self-communication must be explicitly witnessed. This task is carried out by the community which witnesses to Jesus. Rahner implicitly speaks of this community in sacramental terms: it is a community of witnesses "for the salvation of the world (not merely for their own salvation)." In point of fact, Rahner would seem to describe the church in its most essential nature as a community of witness or testimony "that God triumphs by his own doing and victoriously lavishes himself on this humanity and its world."

2° Unity: Foundation for a Constant Witness

Because the witness or testimony of God's victorious love that the community gives must be constant, that is, remaining the same, the community must be one. For the community to be one it must have a cohesiveness and an order. This order must originate from Jesus Christ, because this community witnesses to the victory of God which is precisely accomplished in Jesus Christ. This community is the necessary manifestation of the permanency of God's victory. This community can be large or small, but it can never cease to exist. Rahner underscores the fact that this community does not bear witness to itself — but to God's victory — nor for itself — but for the salvation of the world. This salvation occurs both within and without the community's own circle. In addition, the community cannot take away from anyone her/his vocation to take part in the witness for God, for his Christ, and for the kingdom of God in the process of coming-to-be. The community calls upon all to bring about and to experience for themselves the salvation of the world to which the community bears witness.

c. *The Historical Sociological Dimension of the Community of Witness*

The community of witness necessarily carries out its task historically. Thus the sociological reality of the community is itself an essential element of its existence. Therefore, "if a historical-sociological entity is to exist and endure, the spirit which brought it into being must be embodied in authority," an authority which is able to act, offer unity, and rest upon concrete human beings. The concrete human beings, therefore, in whom this authoriy is embodied, exist from the whole church, and not simply from the concrete part of the church in which their authority is embodied. Similarly, the church only exists inasmuch as it historically manifests itself as one church: sociologically constituted and differentiated in its tasks, authority, and its bearers.

d. The Spirit and Ministerial Office

The word of truth that is proclaimed by the ministerial office of the church always draws its life from faith, a faith which, in the instinct of its Spirit, is lived in the whole church. Similarly, the word of directives and of law in the church are always the manifestations of the impulsive action which the Spirit mediates to the church as a whole. This impulsive action of the Spirit finds itself in the word of ministerial office, of law and of directives. Even the sacramental word in the mouths of the bearers of ministerial office would lose its very essence, if the Spirit would not ensure that, at least in the church as a whole, this sacramental word comes to a faithful fulfillment in those who are receiving the sacrament. All of this Rahner describes as a circle of mutual, reciprocal conditions which cannot be burst apart. This mutual conditioning relationship can only be understood from the perspective of faith.

Equally important to an understanding of Spirit and ministerial office is the affirmation that God's grace is at work in and prevails over history. This victory of God's grace strives for and perseveres in manifesting itself in history and in societal reality. Therefore, so that the victory of Christ is not simply present in Spirit, but in the flesh of history, the bearing of the responsibility of witnessing in the ministerial office of the church to God's victory is itself "grasped" by God's victorious grace. Thus, the bearing of this responsibility, which is brought about by the grace of God, cannot, in any absolute way, fall away from this grace. Naturally, the important emphasis is that this cannot happen in any absolute way, but it is and must be possible for those concrete individuals who bear this responsibility to fall away from God's grace.

Certainly one of the most significant points concerning the relation between the Spirit and ministerial office is made by Vatican II. Rahner underscores the fact that the Council "finds a sacramental and therefore pneumatic basis for the transmission of every ministerial office." This results from the Council declaring that the sacramental ordination of the bishop confers all three ministerial offices: the teaching, sanctifying, and shepherding ministerial offices. Consequently this stresses, insists Rahner, that since "the law is rooted in the Pneuma... it is put into effect and applied in accordance with the will of Christ only when its application is inspired and sustained by this Spirit."[2]

e. Trinitarian Foundation of the Differentiation of Ministerial Office

1° Unity and Difference

The one witness to the victory of God's grace has an inner differentiation. In the first place, the giving of witness itself has various degrees of urgency and various degrees of commitment to witness on the part of human beings and the church. This witness extends not only from that word of ordinary instruction to the word in sacrament, in which what is said itself is allowed to become an event in the concrete life of the individual and the church. Even more so, this historical manifestation of the self-communication of God enters into the authoritative word of the ministerial office of the church specifically in the various dimensions of the church and of human beings.

Rahner sees in the Trinity itself a foundational two-fold differentiation of the historical manifestation of God's self-communication: "the Father utters the eternal Logos of truth and history, and in the breathing of the Spirit of love brings back this self-

---

[2] Rahner, *Pastoral-Theological Observations on Episcopacy in the Teaching of Vatican II* (hereafter *Episcopacy*) in *TI*, Vol. 6, London, 1969, pp. 361-368, esp. p. 363. The significant passage in *LG* regarding episcopal ordination is in n. 21.

utterance — and in it the history in which the Logos is faithfully presented — into the boundless infinity of uncreated God."[3] Consequently, the church's witness to this historical manifestation of God's self-communication is itself absolutely concrete and historical. It is never merely ideology, nor a wordless infinite mysticism, nor merely "otherworldly."

This concrete historical witness of the church has its origin in the "begetting" of the Logos in the flesh — an event which is radically historical — and in the "breathing" of the Spirit. The witness of the church actually realizes the two-fold unity and the one two-foldness which correspond to the "processions," and simultaneously brings them specifically closer to Christian experience.

2° Faith, Hope, and Love

The witness of the ministerial office of the church reflects this unity and difference that is rooted in the Trinity. In its most fundamental aspect, this unity and difference is evidenced by the ministerial office of the church: 1) witnessing to the offer of God's own self, historically manifested in the Logos becoming a human being, thereby calling for faith; 2) witnessing to the victory of this offer in the acceptance of such an invitation by the power of the Holy Spirit of divine love, thereby calling for and obtaining God's love in human beings; and 3) witnessing to the offer of God's self and its acceptance in the midst of this actual ongoing event, thus both calling for and bringing about hope, which itself is the real strength of a still ongoing history. Consequently, ministerial office in the church focuses on faith, love, and hope in human beings, which ministerial office attests is brought about by that which is witnessed to: the victorious self-promise of God to human beings.

Rahner goes on to take this theological reflection on faith, love, and hope as a hermeneutical approach to understanding ministerial office of the church in the traditional three-fold division: teaching, sanctifying, and shepherding-leading. Rahner indicates

[3] Rahner, *Meaning*, p. 25.

that it may be more clarifying to speak of the teaching, sanctifying, and shepherding-leading tasks that make up the one ministerial office. The task of teaching summons the faith of the
bearer. The task of shepherding-leading points to hope for the
conduct of faith, showing the way of the concrete fulfillment of
the still ongoing salvation-history of the individual and of the
church. The task of sanctifying indicates and mediates in the
sacraments ultimately, the event of the grace of love, which unites
one definitively with God and accepts with a radical "yes" the
self-offer of God.

3° *Potestas Iurisdictionis* — *Potestas Ordinis*

This three-fold and one word of witness of the ministerial office
of the church can issue forth to the individual in a two-fold way.
The "teaching" word of truth, the "shepherding-leading" directive toward activity, and the "sanctifying" summons to love, take
place in history, as does the three-fold response of the human
being. On the one hand, this word of witness can be, in general,
intended for the individual insofar as the individual is a member
of the witnessing community. This level is spoken of as *potestas
iurisdictionis* in regard to the authority of the word of the church
in its ministerial office. One may also describe this as the power of
leadership, which includes the general power of teaching. On the
other hand, this word of witness can also be directly intended for
the individual, involving the individual in her/his own unique and
once and for all salvation-response to God's self-promise. This
level is spoken of as *potestas ordinis*, the sanctifying power, the
sacramental authority of the ministerial office of the church.

Rahner insists that these two levels must be seen in their
fundamental unity. He indicates that the Second Vatican Council
has affirmed this unity by declaring that both *potestas iurisdictionis* and *potestas ordinis* are radically communicated in a concrete
way to the bearer in one and the same act, namely the sacrament
of priestly ordination. The significance of this, declares Rahner, is
to confirm that these two powers are, in the deepest way, one and
unique in nature, becoming differentiated from within. They

should not be seen as simply existing side by side, varying from one region to another, as almost disparate from each other. Rather, these two powers are levels of the existential urgency and immediacy of the word of witness of the ministerial office of the church.

2. Ministerial Office: Oneness and Multiplicity

a. The One Original Subject of Full Power in the Church

1° The College of Bishops with its Head

Rahner declares that there can be no doubt that Vatican II's Constitution on the church, *Lumen gentium*, is "the most significant achievement" of the Council. Within *Lumen gentium* he believes that the teaching on the episcopacy is the most important section. One particular aspect of this teaching is of central importance in understanding the meaning of the ministerial office of the church.

The college of bishops "possesses its authority only in union with the Roman Pontiff (*Bischof!*) and under his leadership... But in forming such a college all the bishops are the bearers of full and supreme power in the church." Now, Rahner insists, one of the most essential characteristics which the church proclaims of itself is its unity. Thus, this one church has one goal as well as one task. So it is, necessarily, also one in its ministerial office (*Amt*). It is the college of bishops, united with its head, which is the bearer of this one ministerial office and this one authority upon which this one ministerial office is based.[4]

2° Two Elements of One Fundamental Power

Those who are members of the college of bishops are constituted as members in a two-fold way. On the one hand, this takes

---

[4] Rahner, *The Episcopal Office* (hereafter *Episcopal Office*) in *TI*, Vol. 6, London, 1969, pp. 313-360, esp. pp. 344-345; *On the Relationship between the Pope and the College of Bishops* (hereafter *Pope and College*) in *TI*, Vol. 10, London, 1973, pp. 50-70.

place through a sacramental ordination, through which one is given an authority to sanctify — *potestas ordinis*. On the other hand, through the conferral of pastoral power one is given particular jurisdiction — *potestas iurisdictionis*. Rahner underlines the point that "these two powers (and the ministerial offices which are built upon them and through which they are exercised) must have an inner unity and an ultimately indissoluble connection."[5]

These two powers are fundamentally to be seen as "two elements of one and the same fundamental power." Consequently, if these two powers are joined together with each other as indissoluble in their ultimate root, then "the bearer of this completely one power can only be he who necessarily possesses both. This bearer is the college of bishops under and with the pope."

Rahner offers enlightening reflections concerning the election of the pope with regard to these two powers being irrevocably possessed by the church. The fact that the college of bishops loses the head of the college — normally through death or resignation — does not mean that the church no longer possesses *potestas iurisdictionis* — pastoral power — in a definitive way. The college of bishops carries out its responsibility — at present, through the college of cardinals — to elect a new head of the college. The fact that an election can take place evidences that the college of bishops continues to possess this full pastoral power — with the obligation of electing a new head of the college. Similarly, if an individual is elected the head of the college, and is not a bishop, that person must be ordained bishop. This is so because ultimately in the church and in the college of bishops as a whole, the fullness of pastoral power cannot be separated from *potestas ordinis*: the power of sanctifying.[6]

---

[5] Rahner, *Episcopal Office*, p. 345; "indissoluble union" = unlösliche Verbindung. Rahner stresses that the bearer of this one authority and this one ministerial office is the college of bishops.

[6] Rahner, *Episcopal Office*, pp. 346-347. In a lengthy note, n. 16, pp. 347-348, Rahner further reflects on the possibility of viewing "the act of transmitting the

b. The Division of One Ministerial Office

1° Legitimate Division of an Individual Bishop's Authority

The ministerial office of the individual bishop is "legitimately divided in the church '*vario gradu, variis subiectis*' (priests, deacons)," declares Rahner. This is explicitly stated in *Lumen gentium*. In fact, such a division is to be expected. For, while the college of bishops united with its head is the bearer of full authority in the church, the individual members of the college, as individuals, have only limited authority. Thus, each individual bishop indeed legitimately divides this authority.

As to the historical questions relating to the division of *Ordo* into bishop, priest and deacon, Rahner notes that it is very difficult from the point of view of the history of revelation and of dogma to justify this by *ius divinum*. Therefore, it is indispensable, according to Rahner, to affirm "the fundamental principle that the church can 'divide' the one fullness of *Ordo* according to practical requirements without vitiating (also translatable as: 'abolishing') its sacramentality".

2° Multiplicity of Ministerial Offices: Clergy and Laity

The dividing of this authority by the individual bishop results in "the almost incalculable multiplicity of ministerial offices, functions, authorities and institutions, which exist in the hierarchical church." Rahner goes on to point out that all of this variety is conveyed only very inexactly through the three-fold level of *Ordo*, that is, bishop, priest, and deacon. Yet, it is absolutely essential that all this variety "must be seen and lived as rooted in the pneumatic unity of the sacrament of the episcopal and priestly ministerial office." Consequently, arriving at a conclusion that is of fundamental significance, Rahner declares that every ministerial office in the church is to be seen as spiritual, "as the making concrete of the sacramental mystery of *Ordo*." However, where it is no longer possible for a ministerial office of

supreme pastoral power resident in the pope" as a "grade of the sacrament of order."

the church — whatever may be the task at hand — to be united with the sacrament of *Ordo*, this ministerial office is to be entrusted to laity "who can carry it out just as well or even better."

The important point to emphasize here is that while Rahner strives for achieving as much unity as possible between *potestas ordinis* and *potestas iurisdictionis*, a prior, fundamental principle is that a necessary task is to be carried out regardless of whether one is clergy or lay. This conclusion of Rahner reflects his recognition that it is impossible for any one single individual to be the bearer in a full sense of the *potestas ordinis* and the *potestas iurisdictionis* of the church. Therefore, when there is a task, or a function, a service, or a ministerial office that needs to be carried out for the one well-being of the one church, this fundamentally takes precedence over the attempt to achieve —as much as possible— a unity between *potestas ordinis* and *potestas iurisdictionis*.

3° A Relationship of Tension: the Diocesan Church and the Local Church

Rahner recognizes a certain tension between what he calls the juridical (wrongly rendered in ET as "theoretical"!) and the real structures of the church, specifically in regard to ministerial office. *Lumen gentium* portrays the bishop in such a way that "the whole official action of the church in the transmission of truth and grace is concentrated in him." It would seem, states Rahner, that this image of the bishop is contradicted by reality. Reality presents a picture of the bishop as "a kind of higher administrative official" who only watches over and coordinates the "real and essential work of the church" which is "carried out by the priests in the parish." [7]

---

[7] Rahner, *Episcopacy*, p. 366. This question is very relevant ecumenically: "The Lutheran ecclesiology views the official activity of the church as primarily to be found in the actual preaching of the gospel in the concrete community by the pastor and therefore can only recognize the 'bishop' as the necessary 'superintendent' of this life of the concrete community."

In order to be able to deal with this realistically, Rahner calls for a further development of the theology of the local and particularly the altar community. This theology must affirm that this community is "the manifestation and the actualisation of the church as such at a particular point in space and time." This theology must be made alive and fruitful in the life of the individual community.

To the extent that the local worshipping community does not recognize itself as church but only as "the smallest administrative unit by means of which the universal church (alone) effects the salvation of the individual," to that extent it does not truly understand itself. It is only when the local worshipping community is in reality what it is meant to be, that in turn the "episcopal church" of the diocese is in reality what it is meant to be.

This tension between the diocesan church and the local worshipping community was not evident in the early church. This is simply because "every real local church was an episcopal church." And the problem was not one that occurred in medieval and modern times, because the local worshipping community did not feel itself to be church. But today, there is a recognition that the local worshipping community is the "concrete form of the essence of the church." Thus, that which the church is *iure divino* must be manifested and experienced in the local worshipping community. Only when this happens will "the episcopal nature of the church's essential structure which lies as it were at a deeper level in the organism of the church... become accessible to the religious experience of the Christian and will no longer give the impression of being an abstract theory which has little contact with the concrete life of the church."

4° A Theology of the Local Church

Rahner develops two positive theses regarding the local worshipping community, the parish, as well as some reflections on the limitations of the parish.

a) church as event: necessarily a local community

His first thesis is: "the church, as event, is necessarily a local and localized community." This is based, in turn, on Rahner's conviction "that where the church acts,... it attains a higher degree of actuality than it does by its mere continuing existence." He distinguishes between the church as event, and the church as a "mere institution in its permanent, societal constitution."

The conclusion that Rahner is led to is quite relevant: "where the church makes its appearance and manifests itself precisely insofar as it is a community — that is, a multitude of human beings bound together through a visible event and grace — the church as such reaches a higher degree of event-fullness than it does where an individual endowed with an office actualizes the church by her/his own action in which the other actively co-operating members of the church are not included."

It is in the celebration of the Eucharist, declares Rahner, that the church becomes event most intensively. And an essential characteristic of this "sacramental-cultic act" is, what Rahner names, "placeness": "the Eucharist can be celebrated only by a community which is gathered together in one and the same place." The local, eucharistic worshipping community is not a mere "authorized agency" of one world-church, "the local community is the event of this very universal church itself."

It is also important to keep clearly in mind, as noted above, that "the earliest local church was also an episcopal church." And, consequently, the existence of presbyters must be recognized first and foremost as the plural senate of the local bishop and not a reality that owes its existence to the fact that there were many local communities.

b) Parish: primary realization of the church as event

Rahner's second thesis regarding the parish is: "the parish is the primary realization of the church as event." Nevertheless, it must be affirmed that "local worshipping community" and "parish" are not absolutely identical. Thus, it is quite proper to speak of a monastic community, or a youth group, for example, that comes together for the Eucharist as a local worshipping community. "But, it is the parish which is *de facto* and *de iure* the

primary, most normal and most original form of local community
— and this simply because the parish exists by the principle of
place alone."

The basis of the parish community and its actualization in the
Eucharist is ultimately founded in the bodily, space-time placeness of human beings themselves. This must be recognized as a
necessary condition in which salvation itself takes place, such that
the historical realization of salvation for human beings is a
realization that always necesarily has the characteristic of being
local.

c) Local church: necessary functional character

In spite of its necessary importance, parish, in its theological
meaning, has definite limits. For the local church is realized in the
celebration of the Eucharist even when this celebration is not also
a coming together of the members of a local parish. Thus,
Rahner points to the necessity of distinguishing between two
different realities of placeness: 1) "the placeness of the celebrating
community as such"; and 2) "the generally presupposed common
placeness of those coming together for this Eucharistic celebration." Both of these, in themselves able to be differentiated,
belong together, "because people do not usually come together
for the Mass, as such, if they ordinarily live in different places."
Yet even a celebration of the Eucharist which does not coincide
completely with an existing local community, still manifests "this
presupposed and purely natural commonness of place," because
whenever one exists, one can only exist as "one having a home."
Nevertheless, this fundamental principle of having a home is not
the only principle of the human being's "societalization."

So, the parish "need not be the only form of community which
becomes a real local community in the celebration of the Eucharist." Indeed, the parish cannot be the only local community. For
then, one would be affirming that the universal church only exists
as a "collection of individual local churches or the result of their
subsequent organizational merger." The local church, however,
must be recognized in its necessary functional character "of the

already existing one church of Christ, which... attains its greatest event-fullness in the local community and especially in the local community's celebration of the Eucharist."

A deeper theological appreciation and understanding of the local church will not resolve all the tensions that necessarily exist between the episcopal church and the local church. But a clearer recognition of the mutual relationship that both have towards one another is a step in the church's struggle to realize itself as the one church that it is.

5° Criteria: How to Divide Ministerial Office

The church, as noted above, can divide the one ministerial office "according to practical requirements." But a crucial question concerns the criteria upon which the church makes such decisions. How does the church make such determinations? The response given by Rahner is clearly consistent with his over-all ecclesiology. His considerations on the theology of the local church, given above, provide a necessary framework in which to situate Rahner's response.

It is not possible, declares Rahner, to offer an abstract formal principle that would be valid for all times and in all places. An example of such an approach might be to state as a criterion: the fulfilling of the task of the church. No one could legitimately deny that such a criterion is accurate; but it is, states Rahner, ineffective as a criterion for determining how the one ministerial office of the church should be divided.

The approach at which Rahner arrives, paradoxically expressed as a principle, is this: the principle and the criterion for the concrete form and articulation of church ministerial offices for the proclamation of the Gospel are to be taken from the experimental encounter of the ministerial office with the concrete, general sociological — and by that, the specifically ecclesial — situation.

What Rahner insists upon is the central place that praxis must occupy. Praxis is not "the mere application of prior general principles, but is rather an event of freedom," and consequently the creation of a unique future that has its own autonomy. Praxis is not merely the handmaid of theory. This approach has important consequences in regard to the dividing of the one ministerial office of the church.

The discovery of concrete institutional elements of the church can only occur in concrete experience, in experiment. Consequently, ecclesiology, without losing its own self, exposes itself anew to the forward-pressing sociological situation in which the Gospel must be preached. Rahner stresses that the local community is the focal point where this encounter between ecclesiology and the concrete sociological situation of today takes place. Therefore, it is particularly in the local community that the task of the church, its credibility, and its preaching of the Gospel take place. It is this encounter, this reality that occurs on such a fundamental level — which level Rahner speaks of in terms of a basic community — that becomes extremely important in determining particular ministerial offices of the church.

Rahner recalls, as noted above, that in the early period of the church the community leader "would have been called a bishop." Whereas, from the perspective of patristic theology, bishops today would be more accurately described as "senior" bishops, or metropolitans, or something similar. This has significance that goes far beyond terminology. Rahner questions whether the leader of a local community today has had withdrawn from her/him those tasks, powers, and freedoms which ought to actually befit her/him.

Following from this, Rahner asks whether it is not accurate to predicate what is said theologically about the college of bishops to the college of local pastors. In turn, can one then justifiably view the college of bishops, fundamentally, as the unavoidable organizational representation of the college of pastors. The key point that Rahner makes is that as a basic community becomes more and more the normal type of parish, "then the concrete reality of a diocese and of the episcopal ministerial office must alter too."

As to the practical consequences that this shift has for the leadership of the local community, there are particular details to note. On the one hand, the collaboration between the community and the bishop will necessarily be of a different form than has previously been the case. Secondly, the appointment by the bishop of a leader for the local community is something that takes place in the context of this "new" collaboration. Rahner affirms that the "ordained leader" of the Eucharist and the leader of the community are and should remain identical.

Thus, criteria and principles for determining the division of the one ministerial office are discovered pre-eminently on the level of the local community. And in such community it must emerge experimentally (always including theological reflection, which is indispensable) what structures, and what ministerial offices the community needs. And the community must see that it lives in a vital fraternal and sororal solidarity with other communities — with similar or dissimilar styles. The local community must see what juridical structures are necessary and binding on all the communities for this solidarity.

c. Exhibitive Character of the Ministerial Office's Word of Witness

1° Action of the Church and the Spirit

The word of witness of the ministerial office of the church has, what Rahner calls, an exhibitive character. By this he means that the word does not merely speak "about" something, but it also allows what is said to take place in the human being and to grasp her/him. By definition, this word of witness to God's victorious grace is only authentically a true witness if it comes about and happens both from without and within, from the church and from the Spirit. When, as such, an exhibitive word achieves its most radical fulfillment of itself, involving the church and the individual in a final way, it is proper to speak of this word as a sacramental word. In this perspective, the sacraments as such are the seven-fold "unfolding" of the fulfillment of this word, which is spoken by virtue of the power of order.

Rahner concludes that the authoritative witness of the church to the world that the grace of God is victorious is the one central essence of the hierarchical, ministerial office of the church. By saying this, one does not obscure the sacramental power of the ministerial office, but one recognizes this sacramental power as the most radical case of the ever-exhibitive word of grace. At the same time, one is able from this perspective to see in a more accurate manner the efficacious sacramental action of the ministerial office of the church. This sacramental action concerns a sign-causality.

Thus the grace of God occurs, announcing itself historically and sociologically, through the ministry of sacramental authority. Rahner is very emphatic that this is the only way that one can accurately understand the sacramental action of ministerial office of the church. God's grace, he declares, is not compelled magically, nor is grace restricted to the vicinity of the historical-sociological announcement. In fact, Rahner stresses that the sacramental sign as a historical embodiment of grace is as much an effect as it is a signifying cause.

2° Ministerial Office: Instrumental Cause

All of this means that the ministerial office of the church is the instrumental cause of grace, where grace is manifested as sacramental — and it is this instrumental cause only in the announcing of this grace, and not in any other way. Sacraments, notes Rahner, are not the absolute event of grace, but are the most compacted "case" or "instance" of the historical manifestation of grace in the life of the individual and of the church.

3° Ministerial Office Understood as *Ministerium verbi*

Rahner furthermore indicates that there are two senses in which the terminology *Ministerium verbi* is applicable to the ministerial office of the church. On the one hand, the word spoken by the ministerial office of the church is a word seen as a witness to the world of God's victorious grace. The "world" stands in need of sanctification. But the "world" is present not only outside the church but is also in the church. Thus *Ministe-*

rium verbi can be understood as the function of the ministerial office of the church. On the other hand, the word of witness to God's victorious grace is an accepted witness in the church and a lived witness in all the members of the church. And so, this witness itself is correctly understood as the basic sacrament (*Grundsakrament*) called the church, which is constituted for the salvation of the world —the world being understood as that which is not identical with the church. Thus, in this way, the world experiences the self-offer of God. From this context, *Ministerium verbi* can be understood in a more narrow sense as one particular function of the ministerial office of the church.

d. The Theological Limits of the Ministerial Office of the Church

Introduction

The theological limits of the ministerial office of the church need to be distinguished from its sociological limits. Today, different sociological limits of the church's ministerial office can be noted. One such example is the following. There is a movement from the concept of "popular church" to that of church as "faith community" in the "diaspora or a pluralistic society." As a consequence of this, a bishop, for example, is less able to be supported in the ministerial office of the church through social influence and sociological prestige. For an efficacious carrying out of the ministerial office of the church, a bishop must rely more on a faith and an obedience that are free and are not imposed upon an individual. He must rely upon a brotherly and sisterly love of all the individuals of the church. Such sociological limits are found in the church in every moment of its history. They result from a particular empirical-sociological situation which is subject to historical change. Rahner does not discount these sociological limits as being of no significance. He simply wants to clarify that it is important to also recognize what are the theological limits of the ministerial office of the church, limits which are "unchangeable."

1° Ministerial Office: a Serving Function

The ministerial office of the church has a serving function with regard to the church. This serving function is fundamentally present in every society. For in the church, as in every society, service precedes ministerial office ontologically. (Though this precedence, as in other societies as well, may not always be a temporal precedence).

This serving function of the ministerial office of the church is rooted in an important distinction: the hierarchical structure of the meaning and the goal of a society and the hierarchical structure of the sociological organization of the society are two different things. Rahner declares that a great deal of the antagonism that occurs between clergy and laity is rooted in the failure to recognize this essential distinction.

The exemplification within the church of this distinction is that there is: 1) a hierarchy of ministerial office; and 2) apart from, and before, and above this, a hierarchy of the Spirit, of grace, of solidarity with God , and of holiness. These two are not identical nor even necessarily parallel to each other. Grace is present outside the full and visible association of the Catholic church. Rahner insists that it certainly is not the case that the most important occurrences of grace as well as the historical manifestation of this grace are found only in church as visible society. Ultimately, the fact that there are degrees of the ecclesial-sociological function of the ministerial office of the church does not imply identical degrees of intimacy with God in grace and in love. On the one hand, the ministerial office of the church which "proclaims the authoritative and efficacious word of witness" can be considered as nearness to Christ and to God. On the other hand, the intimacy on which this word of witness depends in the most profound way, that is, the self-communication of God in the Spirit, is not an exclusive prerogative of the clergy. [8]

[8] Rahner, *Meaning*, p. 31. The ET fails to translate the fact that God is the intimacy on which the word of witness of the ministerial office of the church depends. The ET loosely states: "but the intimacy which is really all that matters at the end of the day…" The original clearly refers God to the "word of witness".

Nevertheless, Rahner is very clear that although the clergy's bearing witness to the intimacy of God cannot be identical with that intimacy, that person is most unfortunate who bears witness to what one does not personally possess. Such a person is "a sounding brass and a tinkling cymbal." Thus Rahner realistically points to the fact that there are indeed "occupational hazards" for one who shares in the ministerial office of the church: 1) the temptation to arrogance; 2) to empty institutionalism; 3) to mere religious routine; 4) to striving for power; 5) to legalism. All of this, in effect, is the terrible state of affairs that results from perverting the true nature of religion.

The one who holds ministerial office in the church must exemplify the serving function that specifies ministerial office itself. The meaning and goal of the society of the church is the self-communication of God with human beings. Therefore, the individual is most eminently a person of the church "who loves God most unselfishly, who most steadfastly carries the cross of existence as Christ's cross." To fail to see this is to reduce the church to a mere sociological religion-organization. But because the very meaning and goal of the church is much more than this, those who hold ministerial office in the church must serve the church in its fullest sense. For it is not a mere outward orderliness function, but a mediating of salvation in truth and grace that comprises the ministerial office of the church.

Both laity and clergy must recognize this fundamental serving function of the ministerial office of the church in regard to the mediating of salvation. Then, the distinction between "hierarchy of ministerial office" and "hierarchy of intimacy with God" must be accepted and affirmed. The laity must recognize that these two cannot be "confused" with one another. They are not identical. The clergy must recognize that the two are fundamentally inseparable from each other. The reality, according to Rahner, is that there is an insoluble interpenetration of the two, so that clergy and laity alike should humbly praise God's free grace. This is an important understanding of a theological limit of the ministerial office of the church.

2° Ministerial Office and the "Hierarchy" of Free Charisms

A second theological limit of the ministerial office of the church is seen in the necessary distinction between the "hierarchy" of ministerial office and the "hierarchy" of free charisms in the church. Not only is there a necessary distinction to be made between the "hierarchy" of ministerial office and the "hierarchy" of intimacy with God, but one must distinguish between the "hierarchy" of ministerial office and the "hierarchy" of free charisms. This is so because in addition to recognizing that the clergy do not have an exclusive prerogative with regard to intimacy with God, neither are clergy the sole bearers of the actual fulfillment and coming-to-be of the church as such.

Free charisms are present in the church, as charisms bestowed by God, which are aimed at the church and its activity, and which belong to the permanent nature of the church. The individuals who are the bearers of these charisms — a determination which is the result of the free grace-choice of God — are, or can be, all individuals in the church and not only the clergy.

It is important to note that Rahner focuses on the action of God as the distinctive criterion. God's action alone is fundamental. The distinction between the "hierarchy" of ministerial office and the "hierarchy" of the charisms is rooted in God's own free action. Consequently, Rahner does *not* look for a fundamental distinction that is drawn from a number of other factors, such as: 1) laity can administer the most fundamental sacrament of baptism, and can also actively consummate the sacrament of marriage; 2) laity, through their instinctive faith, through their common priesthood, through their world-mission and their shaping the world, are active bearers of the fulfillment and coming-to-be of the church; 3) the love and the patience of the laity, that is, as individuals of the church, which love and patience they embody in the most essential way in daily Christian living, belong to the very life and fulfillment of the church — that is, the element of the institution, the aspect of teaching, and the reality of ministerial office are not the only things which belong to the life and fulfillment of the church.

While it is necessary, therefore, to distinguish free charisms from ministerial office, it is certainly possible for charisms to be bestowed upon those who hold ministerial office. The important point is that wherever free charisms are present, either in those who hold ministerial office, or in those who do not, these charisms must be respected by the ministerial office of the church. Those in ministerial office must understand that without the charismatic element in the church, the life of the church would turn into a bureaucratic business, losing the radiance of holiness and strength for the future.

The ministerial office of the church, with respect to the life of the church in faith, hope, and love, has a regulatory function, the tasks of fostering life, of steering, and of protecting against false proliferations. If the life of the church were not actually living, if its liveliness were not permitted the necessary freedom and room, then ministerial office would necessarily turn into the meticulous order of a mortuary. However, Rahner notes that such a reality is quite problematic, if only because it is denied to no one who holds ministerial office in the church to be a life-witnessing charismatic. Those who are draw attention to the essentials, protect against an over-estimation of individual functions, warn against an overdone institutionalization, and urge that enough room be permitted for other functions.

Rahner declares that some wish to de-emphasize free charisms in the church by pointing out that the sacramental function of ministerial office in the church not only regulates life but actually begets life. But, while certainly in the sacrament there occurs the begetting of divine life, it is presupposed that the receiver of the sacrament has the necessary "disposition." The awakening of this enlivening disposition does not rest solely with the sacramental power of ministerial office. It itself is, as well, fundamentally an effect of the charismatic liveliness of all the members of the church in which the receiver of the sacrament lives or into which s/he is entering.

The emphatic conclusion that Rahner reaches regarding ministerial office of the church and the "hierarchy" of free charisms is that ministerial office is not the Lord of the Spirit and the Spirit's charisms, but its servant. While it is true that an individual in the church can, through sin, pervert a genuine charism, the ministerial office of the church can also be guilty of this perversion through cold-heartedness and bureaucratic routine.

God alone is the one who builds up one church out of the necessary antagonism and pluralism of spirits, tasks, and services. And Rahner indicates that ministerial office must not be surprised or indignant if something stirs in the life of the Spirit before it has been planned in the ministries of the church. On the other side of the question, the faithful must not imagine that they have nothing to do until an order comes from above. There are things that God wills and asks of the conscience of the individual well before there has been a sign to begin coming from the ministerial office of the church — even concerning trajectories that have not yet been approved and established.

3° Ministerial Office and Sin and Inadequacy

A third theological limit of the ministerial office of the church is the inadequacy and sinfulness of those who hold ministerial office in the church. Because ministerial office is a permanent authority of the church, its very permanency does not simply exclude, but actually positively allows a number of things to be included. Rahner lists some examples.

1) Through human inadequacy and also through sin, that which is taught and preached in the church may be rash and inadequate, because that which is old is judged as being not useful for improving things today, simply because that which is old is something traditional and venerable. 2) The signs of the times may not be understood, and opportune moments may be missed, as again and again a light goes out under the candle-snuffer of bureaucratic routine and a petty legalism. 3) The machinery may forget that it only has meaning inasmuch as it awakens faith, hope and love in people's hearts. In these examples, Rahner indicates that the authority of ministerial office will always expect too much of the one who holds ministerial office,

making that person "painfully aware that however true our doctrine, however valid the administration of the sacraments may be, inwardly we remain in an imbalance toward (our) received task."

Rahner describes those who hold the ministerial office of the church as little, poor servants of God, who, as bearers of ministerial office, are poor, sinful human beings. For they are messengers of the truth of Christ, but they must beforehand be hearers of his word. They always remain people who are tempted by unbelief. They themselves must receive the sacraments of Christ which they administer. In regard to these sacraments, the bearer of ministerial office has no ultimate certainty whether one has "really opened the inmost chamber of her/his heart so that God's grace may enter in."

To emphasize the church's indestructability does not change the fact that God cannot only safeguard his truth through the triumph of the one who bears witness to that truth. God can safeguard his truth even if the one who bears witness to it dies, or fails in other ways, such as through inadequacy and sin. The one who bears witness may write with crooked lines, though without the lines themselves actually being crooked. Whatever victory of God's grace takes place in the church, remains God's victory. It is not the result of the triumph of the one who holds ministerial office in the church. Those who are bearers of the ministerial office of the church are not owners of God and God's grace-filled self-gift as such. Rather, they bear witness in an efficacious word to this God of grace in Christ. "And therefore even as such witnesses they can be sinful human beings."

4° Ministerial Office and Personal Responsibility

A fourth theological limit the ministerial office of the church has is that border which begins with each one's own heart. Every individual must take the ultimate concrete decisions of her/his conscience — which are for salvation or non-salvation — in ultimate solitariness. When an individual goes from the general norm that is applicable to a particular decision and moves to a concrete action based on one's own conscious decision, that individual must be responsible to God alone.

Rahner notes three specific examples that focus on the relationship between the ministerial office of the church and the personally responsible individual. First, each one "must meet Christ in her/his neighbor: it is not enough for the priest to give her/him the body of Christ in communion if s/he does not find Christ in her/his sister and brother." Secondly, each one "must die her/his death, even though the priest gives her/him the church's viaticum for her/his journey into the final silence." A third example is that each one must be a witness to the grace of God in the everydayness of life, even though the community of witnesses, the church, has an official ministerial representative of this witness.

The importance of personal responsibility has consequences for the necessity of criticism. Rahner declares that criticism and a critical public opinion are necessary today in the church, but, unless the people of the church, and those who hold ministerial office in the church, love the church through loyal service, what is offered as criticism will lack authenticity. Criticism without love is not a virtue. Both those who hold ministerial office in the church as well as those who do not hold ministerial office "make the church a church of sinners."

Much of the lay criticism of the ministerial office of the church actually arises from a "clericalist theology" which declares that those who hold ministerial office in the church must be angels and may not be human beings. In contrast to this theology, recognizing and accepting the humanness of all who make up the church is essential. On the part of the bearer of ministerial office, that individual must acknowledge the great strain of ministerial office and one's own inadequacies. On the part of the one who does not bear the responsibility of ministerial office, one must endure for oneself the unavoidable humanness of the one in ministerial office. The only difference in terms of the humanness of the two is that the humanness of the one who is not a bearer of ministerial office may manifest itself less harshly. "Each must have patience with the other."

In contrast with what God alone must and may do, what ministerial office in the church does and can do is quite modest. There is first and foremost the fulfillment of salvation, and secondly there is the mediation of salvation through word and sacrament. The two are not identical, but neither are they able to be completely separated. Rahner emphasizes that salvation does occur without the mediation of the ministerial office of the church. Yet, this ministerial office has an essential and necessary place in the order of salvation. Rahner expresses the importance of the ministerial office of the church in a simple comparison: ministerial office belongs to, if one may say so, "the flesh of Christ, without which there is no salvation."

Thus, even where the church, in its ministerial office, would not efficaciously mediate salvation to the individual through the church's faith-creating word or its sacrament, the church still remains the great historical basic sacrament. As this basic sacrament, it specifically shows in an historical manifestation the salvation of this individual. For the church is, after all, the eschatological basic sacrament of salvation of the world.[9]

e. Conclusion

Rahner views the church as a family. The proper relationship between the bearers of the ministerial office of the church and the other members in the people of God in the church depends upon a number of factors. An essential factor is that the church is fundamentally one, and so its oneness must be ever realized. Consequently there is a necessity for all who make up the church to serve in a self-less manner the one well-being of the church. The essential question that each individual will have to answer is not concerning one's place in the sociological structure of the church, but about one's faith, hope and love. Both clergy and

---

[9] Rahner, *Meaning*, p. 43. The ET inexactly translates *die Kirche in ihrem Amt* as "church office." Rahner declares that it is the church, in its ministerial office, that efficaciously mediates salvation. The ecclesiological context of ministerial office cannot be neglected or minimized.

laity are in the same service of God. Both must give witness, in their own place, to the grace of God which is meant for all human beings.

Within such a framework, Rahner sees it as possible for the laity first to affirm that the community of witness to the grace of God for the world must have an order. Secondly, laity can affirm that there must be bearers of the ministerial office of the church who declare this word of witness to the world, the world that is found inside as well as outside the church. Thirdly, and consequently, laity can give the obedience that is due to those in ministerial office in the area of their competence, and give them patient, brotherly and sisterly love.

On the part of those who are bearers of the ministerial office of the church, they can affirm that they are nothing other than servants of this word of witness, the content of which belongs to everyone in the church. It is God who communicates himself to all in grace.

Rahner sees no room for anti-clerical or anti-lay feelings. For the "signs of the time" indicate that the only effective significance of the ministerial office of the church is such that it draws its life from the free faith-obedience and the brotherly and sisterly love of all the members of the church. Consequently, when an individual takes upon oneself the burden of ministerial office of the church — which brings no earthly honor nor worldly advantage — every believer will be happy and thankful to God.

The ministerial office of the church is not something which will last forever. Vatican II, Rahner notes, declares that "the pilgrim church in her sacraments and institutions, which pertain to this present time, takes on the appearance of this passing world." The ministerial office of the church will come to an end, because it has carried out its service. But that to which the ministerial office of the church bears witness — which it mediates in the efficacious word of witness — is eternal, indeed, is God's own self. Therefore, all those who bear the ministerial office of the church must keep before them the words of Paul: "For what we preach is not ourselves, but Jesus Christ as Lord, with ourselves as your servants for Jesus' sake... But we have this treasure in earthen vessels, to show that the transcendent power belongs to God and not to us" (2 Cor 4:5,7; RSV).

What is fundamental for finding the true position of the ministerial office of the church is to "discover the infinite in the finite," to discover God in the human being, not so that the two turn into one, but also so that the two are not separated. Keeping this in mind, one can affirm that the bearer of ministerial office deserves a more mature obedience, others' confidence, and "a little compassion because of the crushing and painful responsibility" that one bears. At the same time, believers must affirm that the bearer of the ministerial office of the church is not the Lord of one's faith, hope, and love, but the servant of God, the servant of our joy, which is to be the ones redeemed by God.

3. Episcopal Ministerial Office and Sacramentology

The previous two sections of this chapter have centered on the meaning of the ministerial office of the church in its unity and its multiplicity. The ministerial office of the church does not exist in the abstract, but only by means of the concrete lives of individual human beings. Consequently, some elements of the episcopal ministerial office of the church have already been seen. In what follows, this episcopal ministerial office of the church is looked at more specifically —particularly from the perspective of sacramentology.

a. College of Bishops: Reflecting the Reality of the Church

Vatican II, comments Rahner, reaffirms that the bishops, as successors of the apostles, are those "in the first place" who are the bearers of ministerial offices and a concomitant holy authority, which authority must be seen fundamentally as service. Bishops are necessarily "under the pope"; he is the visible principle and foundation "of the unity of the episcopate."[10]

[10] Rahner, *Episcopacy*, p. 361. Rahner's reference is to *LG*, n. 18. See, also, Rahner, *Pope and College*, pp. 60-61: "The Second Vatican Council makes no attempt to derive the plenary power of the college of bishops from the plenary

This subject, the college of bishops with and under the pope, of the highest leadership in the church must mirror the peculiarity of this church. The peculiarity of the church first of all appears in this: unity becomes visible in a multiplicity, and multiplicity becomes visible in unity. This is particularly valid if one affirms the church as the "sacrament" of love in the world. For if the church, out of its most inner nature, unites differences, at the same time it affirms and enters into its own diversity. Similarly, there is the reality of unity and of differentiation concerning the church: there is the multiplicity of the effecting of salvation in unique freedom for the individual, and at the same time there is the "covenant", the community , in which the individual finds the mediation of salvation. If the bearer of full authority of leadership in the church is to repeat and represent this reality of the church, then this must be both collegial and personal in the one bearer.

b. The Pope: Head of the College — Member of the Church

Only in Christ is there a coinciding per se of the personal aspect and the official ministerial, that is, functional, aspect. In a member of the church — who is redeemed — these two do not perfectly coincide. Consequently, even though the pope is correctly seen as the visible "representation" on earth of Christ, the pope is always a member of the church and stands on the side of the church. The pope, Rahner states, "is head of the church precisely inasmuch as he is head of the college of bishops."[11] It is precisely because the pope has the function as head of the college of bishops that he represents in his one self "both the unity of the church and her diversity", in which the church is formed together from many churches. The pope, as a ministerial office person, is a member of the church and the head of the college of bishops.

power of its head." It traces back this power to the succession of the episcopacy from the Apostolic College and recognizes this power to be bestowed by Christ to the College itself and not to Peter as such.

[11] Rahner, *Pope and College*, p. 66.

Therefore, "his personal action is still an act of the bearer of the ministerial office as such."

c. *Individual Bishops: Ministerial Office "in the name of Christ"*

By virtue of one's membership in the college of bishops an individual bishop fundamentally bears the responsibility of episcopal ministerial office "in the name of Christ and not that of the pope." The episcopal ministerial office is not something which is delegated.

This declaration of Vatican II is enormously important. For it clearly repudiates the idea — which Rahner indicates has been very prevalent among clergy and laity alike — "that a bishop is nothing more than a subordinate official of the pope." An individual bishop not only bears a responsibility and a task for a particular aspect of the church's life, but, as an individual member of the college of bishops, bears a responsibility and a task for the whole church. (An individual bishop, as individual, does not possess jurisdiction for the whole church. This belongs to the bishop of Rome, though not as an individual, but as the head of the college of bishops, that is, as pope.)

d. *Particular Episcopal Ministerial Office*

1° Necessity of Wider Groupings of Bishops

Consequently, the witness to and responsibility for unity — the one faith, life and mission of the church — belongs in an essential way to the college of bishops. The challenge is how the college of bishops carries this out. This responsibility and task for unity can be seen in a sacramental context. For Rahner notes that "the unity of the college and of its task manifests itself and results in unity in the practical order by wider ecclesiastical units (patriarchates, etc.) and today also in bishops' conferences..."

The college of bishops exists as one college as a result of the action of the Spirit. But, because the college is made up of individual human beings, its unity is a unity in plurality. This, too, evidences a sacramental dimension: the unity is only achieved through — and not in spite of — the plurality. Thus the grouping together of individual bishops into "working units" serves the whole college of bishops in its one responsibility. The unity which is signified manifests and results in unity.

Because this unity of the college of bishops is not simply a given static reality, but is an event which must be continually realized, ways must ever be found for the fuller realization of this collegial unity.

2° Co-workers in the Papal Ministerial Office: Bishops and Cardinal Bishops

A concern that Rahner voices is "the need for the pope to be supported in the government of the universal church through representatives of the bishops of the whole church."[12] A key element in Rahner's suggestion is that those bishops who carry out this task should not reside permanently in Rome: "otherwise they will only become Roman curial officials or agents for bishops or bishops' conferences without any initiative or responsibility of their own."

This same basic theme emerges for Rahner in regard to the college of cardinals. "From the viewpoint of purely systematic thought it would seem obvious that the representatives of the whole church should elect its head."[13] However, it must be conceded that the whole college of bishops is able to exercise this task in a practical way only by establishing a type of electoral committee. And so, concludes Rahner, we are "back again at some kind of a college of cardinals."

Consequently, the decision of Pope John XXIII to ordain as bishops all the cardinals of the Curia who were not already bishops is one which Rahner himself supports. The foundation of Rahner's agreement with the action of John XXIII is fundamentally from a sacramental perspective. Ordaining these individuals as bishops gives a sacramental ground to the fact that these non-episcopal cardinals juridically and in practice belong to the leadership college of the church. As to the criticism that it is only

---

[12] Rahner, *Episcopacy*, p. 365.
[13] Rahner, *Episcopal Office*, p. 325.

proper for an individual bishop to be a local bishop, Rahner responds in a surprisingly strong way. He declares that whoever de facto "participates in the highest governing body of the church shall also have the sacramental authorization and grace of state" (more exactly: "grace of ministerial office"!).

It is precisely this concern for recognizing and affirming the sacramental foundation of the ministerial office of the church that leads Rahner to far-reaching conclusions.

3° Titular Bishops

Rahner looks specifically to the reality of titular bishops. These are individuals, he declares, who have been entrusted with a ministerial office and definite tasks such that these tasks which constitute this ministerial office make it appropriate and meaningful for the bearer to be "a member of the supreme governing college of the church." Rahner emphasizes that there certainly are ministerial offices of the church which — by their importance — correspond to the responsibility exercised by the college of bishops.

Titular bishops, in practice, exemplify that the territorial principle is an important one in the church, but "it is not the only structural principle." It would be false to assume that only local bishops may constitute the college of bishops.

Rahner suggests, therefore, that it would be most meaningful for the highest and permanent leaders of the large religious Orders to be titular bishops. Though not adverting to the possibility as such, Rahner's suggestion would appear valid in regard to both men and women leaders. The significant criteria would be more in terms of the actual responsibility and tasks that are given to the leader.

A particular objection to ordaining as bishops such leaders of religious Orders is the fact that this leadership position is not always a life-time position. Nevertheless, Rahner questions whether the duration that one holds such a significant ministerial office of the church is an objectively sufficient reason for not ordaining such a person a bishop.

4° Auxiliary Bishops

Rahner also looks at the reality of auxiliary bishops. He makes the emphatic assertion that to ordain an individual a bishop primarily or exclusively as a celebrant of the sacrament of confirmation does not justify that such a person should be a member of the apostolic college of bishops. "Even a simple priest is sacramentally empowered... to administer confirmation validly and licitly." On the other hand, in the case of large dioceses which on good grounds cannot be meaningfully divided, a "second" bishop is appropriate in the ministerial office of auxiliary bishop. The many tasks of such a bishop and one's consequent importance that goes beyond the local diocese, justify that this individual be a member of the college of bishops — and, therefore, an individual bishop. Rahner sees the necessity of a principle of proportionality relating to what particular local tasks are commensurate with one being a member of the college of bishops.

5° The Local Bishop
a) Episcopal ordination always "relative" not "absolute"

The difference between relative and absolute ordination in regard to a bishop is well known, states Rahner. A relative ordination is the ordaining of an individual as bishop "for a determined church as its local bishop". In an absolute ordination, an individual is ordained a bishop without any such relationship. However, the very fact that "a titular see '*in partibus infidelium*' is given to a bishop who is not ordained as a local bishop 'is a constant reminder that in itself relative ordination is the normal case.'" Rahner, however, reaches a further conclusion.

The college of bishops, with and under the pope, is one. The function which this one college exercises is likewise one. When an individual becomes a member of the college of bishops, that is, becomes a bishop, that individual is not only the bearer of the *potestas ordinis*, the power of order, but also the bearer of the *potestas iurisdictionis*, the power of jurisdiction (or pastoral power). These two powers are not capable of being completely lost from one another. Thus Rahner concludes that "theologically there cannot be a purely 'absolute' ordination in any unqualified sense."

Rahner points out that this conclusion corresponds to a related, though distinct, theological position. It is, namely, the growing conviction that the ordination itself — in this case, as a bishop — does not confer "any radical sacramentally grounded and formed faculty for the exercise of pastoral power." And this understanding, Rahner indicates, is expressed in most of the ordination liturgies of different churches. The pastoral power that one exercises as a bishop would seem to be rooted, therefore, in the fact that an individual — through the visible ordination rite — becomes a member of the college of bishops. There is no extraordinary and direct change that takes place in the individual as individual, but insofar as the individual now belongs to the college of bishops. Although Rahner does not explicitly state this, his consideration would seem applicable in an analogous way to the ordinations of priest and deacon.

With regard, therefore, to the distinction between the absolute and relative ordination of a bishop, Rahner emphasizes that what is commonly or merely juridically described as "relative ordination" is, in actuality, "a particular species of relative ordination, namely that in which is conferred also the ministerial office of local bishop." Therefore both a relative and an absolute ordination of a bishop "relates to, is relative to, a ministerial office." If an individual is ordained a bishop and thus shares in the one pastoral power of the college of bishops and is also entrusted with a real episcopal ministerial office of the church — though not the ministerial office of local bishop — one is led to describe this ordination as a relative ordination.[14]

Membership in the college of bishops is such that each individual member is not a member in the same way. There are different levels and ways that membership occurs. Thus, "a titular bishop does not have to be, nor is, a member of the episcopal

[14] Rahner, *Episcopal Office*, p. 331.

college in precisely the same sense as a residential bishop."[15] The important consideration can be expressed in terms of an adequate proportionality: "a relative ordination, therefore, which would be desirable from every point of view would be one in which someone receives a ministerial office or in which someone's ministerial office is sacramentally consecrated which truly qualifies her/him to be a suitable member of the college of bishops."[16] On the other hand, an ordination would be undesirable if, apart from the membership in the college of bishops and the "mere power of Order", there would be no function, discovered or bestowed, which would make the bearer of the episcopal ministerial office — in its significance for the whole church — "homologous" to a local Ordinary.

b) Local episcopal ministerial office and the diocese

In many ways, Rahner's reflections on the local bishop, and hence, the diocese, are the "other side of the coin" from his considerations on the local worshipping community. As seen above, there is a tension between the *Bischofskirche* and the *Ortskirche*. It can be helpful now to study this tension more from the perspective of the *Bischofskirche*, the episcopal church.

It is not an easy question to determine how many local worshipping communities ought to compose a diocese. The ancient local diocese existed in a sociological setting of the Polis-state (city-state). The modern-day province diocese is rather situated in the sociological setting of the region-state. This serves to stress the fact that while the diocese fundamentally is to be "a

[15] Rahner, *Episcopal Office*, p. 332. For example, "while titular bishops can be and are members of the Council, they are not necessarily so." For a Council, which is not *ius divinum*, demands a "representation of the college of bishops" and not "a physical completeness in the number of the assembled bishops." Rahner makes an additional comparison with baptism. Baptism constitutes a certain, though not full, membership in the church if the one baptized is a heretic or a schismatic. Similarly, if an individual is validly ordained a bishop, the one ordained belongs to the college of bishops in a certain, though not full way, if the individual bishop is a heretic or a schismatic (p. 332, n. 7).

[16] Rahner, *Episcopal Office*, p. 333.

real representation of the life of the universal church," the form
of the diocese "is subject to historical change."

A basic premise with which Rahner begins is that a diocese
"should not be too small." This premise follows from his observation about the institutional element of the church today. The
"apparatus" of the institutional element of the church is today
situated in the context of an ever more complex technology and
the reality of a "faceless society." In this setting, the "objectively
correct trend is tending to an increase rather than a decrease in
the size of dioceses."

One area in which this is particularly evident is in regard to
training individuals for the pastoral work of the church. This
takes place in established pastoral institutes and other places of
training for those who are being prepared for the most varied
ministerial offices of the church that are by their nature suppor-
tive ministerial offices.

Rahner sees the large diocese becoming more and more the
normal type of diocese, in large measure because "the city is
becoming increasingly the normal domicile." But is this theologically justified? Rahner believes it is. His reasoning is interesting,
as he argues by means of negative limits.

A bishop of a "miniature diocese" of a few thousand individuals has no justified claim to be a member of the highest college
of leadership for the whole church. Such a bishop would be one
in name, but in terms of actual practice would be exercising the
ministerial office of a dean who has the authority to celebrate
confirmation. Ultimately, Rahner insists upon a certain proportionality. He seems to be more willing to set some type of limit in
terms of how many individual members actually constitute the
college of bishops. He does not see it as possible to multiply
indefinitely the number of bishops. Otherwise, he states, the
consequence would be that only individuals who are senior
bishops, patriarchs, metropolitans, presidents of bishops' conferences, and so forth, would be true bishops. The leader of such a
small diocese would not any longer have that which makes a
territorial district into a "church."

Rahner speaks of a diocese as a member-church. The leader of this member-church should be a member of the college of bishops. And the member-church must be a church that is representative for the whole church. This means that "a proper diocese must also be to a sufficient extent the bearer of such functions as necessarily belong to the universal church apart from the eucharistic celebration and the proclamation of the word."[17]

This necessitates, if it is to be effective, that such a larger diocese have intermediate structures that are developed "from below." The principle of subsidiarity applies to the member-church in a pre-eminent way. Present structures already in existence, such as deaneries, need to be made use of in a sufficient way. Other structures must be developed.

From a negative perspective, if a diocese fails to develop itself, appropriately using the principle of subsidiarity, it would be understandable that one would long for a smaller diocese. If, however, such a small diocese is the result of a failure to develop a truly effective larger diocese, the head of such a small diocese would spiritually, sociologically, and particularly ecclesially be seen as "a parish priest who administers confirmation and is able to ordain priests." The *potestas iurisdictionis* of a local bishop must correspond to a field of activity which is worthy of its importance.

e. Sacraments and Ministerial Office Fundamentally Collegial

Through episcopal ordination, a bishop shares in the "one and full power which is originally present in the college of bishops as united with its head the pope." Consequently, the pope is not only the visible principle of the unity of the college of bishops with respect to the *potestas iurisdictionis*, but also with respect to

---

[17] Rahner, *Episcopal Office*, pp. 336, 339. Rahner cites a number of functions that should be exercised in a real diocesan church, among these: a seminary for priestly formation, an educational system, charitable organizations, the influencing of public opinion, etc. Without these the spiritual life cannot be supported by a diocese.

the *potestas ordinis*. The pope appears as the highest and unique bearer of the *potestas ordinis*. Now this does not mean, cautions Rahner, that the pope "needs to be able to perform more individual sacramental acts than any other bishop, or to perform them with greater intensity." Rather, as pope "he represents the unity of sacramental power in the church." Thus, this rooting of the *potestas ordinis* in the combined college of bishops allows one to understand that all administration of sacraments can be — if not must be — "collegial acts".[18]

Rahner cites a number of examples. When the concelebration of the Eucharist takes place, this is a fundamental collegial act. Concelebration must be understood "not as a synchronisation of many masses, but as one single sacrifice specifically in the dimension of the sacramental sign." The collegial character of the sacrament of reconciliation in the early church is very apparent. The bishop, together with the presbyterium, granted the *pax* with the church through the laying on of hands. This act can be understood, notes Rahner, thoroughly as a collegial act, notwithstanding that its collegial character is not based on an act of the combined college of bishops, but of the college of the bishop and his presbyterium. A third example is the Easter anointing of the sick in as much as this was administered by several priests.

These examples all lend support to the premise of the fundamental possibility of a "collegial act" specifically in the carrying out of a sacrament. Consequently, it is possible to conclude: the church establishes a sacramental sign as hierarchically constituted, and its sacramental activity, corresponding to the nature of the church, is always an act as such of the church and its college. Therefore, this sacramental activity is either established as an actual "collegial act," or as the act of an individual who is but sharing in the sacramental power of the church, and so carries out this sacramental activity in the name of the church.

The position which Rahner presents in regard to ministerial office and sacramentology clearly calls for affirming that they

---

[18] Rahner, *Pope and College*, p. 68.

cannot be completely separated from each other, nor completely confused — that is, mixed — with each other. A particularly important conclusion is to recognize the fundamental collegial character of all sacramental activity of the church. This follows from the fact that *potestas ordinis* is originally and fundamentally borne by the one subject, the college of bishops with and under the pope. Thus, the relationship between the episcopal ministerial office and sacramentology cannot be minimized. In turn, the fact that the *potestas ordinis* together with the *potestas iurisdictionis* are elements of the one power borne by the college of bishops emphasizes the pneumatic or sacramental character that marks the *potestas iurisdictionis* itself.

CHAPTER II

FURTHER SHARING
IN THE ONE MINISTERIAL OFFICE

1. Priestly Ministerial Office

a. Fundamental Terminology

1° Highly Significant and Important Functions

Tradition and current usage, notes Rahner, employ the term "priestly" to refer to the leadership function of the Eucharistic celebration and the sacramental forgiveness of sins — along with the administration of the anointing of the sick. Therefore, a particular function that is recognized today as being of high significance and importance in the church should only be described as "priestly" if it includes these traditionally designated "priestly" functions of the leadership of the Eucharist, the forgiveness of sins and the anointing of the sick. [1]

For Rahner, this statement is far from being primarily based on terminological considerations. For he affirms that it is possible for the church to so divide the one ministerial office recognizing that 1) the concept 'priesthood' can cover varying official ministerial and sacramentally conferred functions, and 2) that there can be other sacramentally conferred "significant and important" functions apart from the priesthood (the original may also be rendered: "next to" or "beside" the priesthood) for example, the function of "teacher," and the function of "community leader." Rahner emphasizes that it is not church dogma that only the conferral of the ministerial office of bishop, priest, and deacon

---

[1] Rahner, *The Point of Departure in Theology for Determining the Nature of the Priestly Office* (hereafter *Departure*) in *TI*, Vol. 12, London, 1974, pp. 31-38, esp. pp. 32, 35.

can be a sacrament. This much broader approach to ministerial office and sacrament is exemplified in the medieval theological position with regard to "minor orders."

An additional consideration is the recognition that the "content" itself of the episcopal, priestly, and diaconal ministerial offices remains an open question with respect to the New Testament and later periods. Yet, even presupposing a three-fold division into the "classic" ministerial offices, one is still able to affirm that there can be other genuine, ever-new historically necessitated divisions of this one ministerial office. It is clear, states Rahner, that both next to and within the three-fold division of ministerial office, history is acquainted with many other ministerial office functions and the individuals who are the bearers of these.

2° Concepts of Priest and Prophet

Rahner also reflects on the term priest and prophet. Priestly activity — in the context of pre-Christian religious philosophy — is described as "the visible, cultic expression (in sacrifice and prayer) of the inner religious attitude of the human being; it is accordingly in itself the visibility of a relationship to God established by the human being." Accordingly Rahner concludes that the priesthood "belongs to the normal, enduring institutions of human life," and that priestly activity, that is, sacrifice, can be carried out in an original way by every normal authority of human society. Historically, this means that priestly activity, tied to already existing authority structures, has been primarily, if not exclusively, limited to men.

'Prophethood' is concerned with "a new relationship between God and human beings which is established by God." Prophetic activity is rooted in the self-revelation of God. Thus Rahner clearly contrasts priestly activity, the visibility of the human word to God, from prophetic activity, the visibility of God's word to human beings. While priestly activity is expressed within the context of established human structures, prophetic activity is not so able to be organized in institutional ways. It also means that — specifically from the perspective of history — prophetic activity can be carried out by a woman, who "can also be bearer of the prophetic spirit."

Rahner notes that both concepts have significantly influenced one another in many ways. For example, a prophetic revelation may indicate the establishment of sacrifice in a particular concrete form. It is, however, also possible for the two concepts to simply be seen as coinciding. If this happens the result is that the priest is conceived as a magician, and the prophet as a fortune teller. Therefore, it is important to carefully distinguish priestly from prophetic activity. Priestly activity is the expression "from below" of the posture toward God that human beings take up within the framework of human life. While prophetic activity, in so far as it really occurs, is the expression "from above" of God's revealing word which is not situated in the framework of human life, it is "above" human experience. It is very important to note, however, that within the context of Christianity, the concepts of priest and prophet are transformed.

The cultic priesthood of Christianity is only a "serving" priesthood "for and in the priesthood and sacrificial act of Christ. The power of Christian cultic activity is the rendering-present sacramentally of the historical salvation-reality of Christ." It possesses eschatological exclusiveness and finality, and so no sacrifice and no grace is possible outside of it. Rahner emphatically insists that this priestly ministerial activity does not bring about God's saving will towards humanity nor establish God's reconciliation and its acceptance in Christian worship. Rather, this activity only constitutes all this, that is, salvation-reality, as present for us as an ever-new sacramental-historical reality of our lives.

Priestly ministerial activity is thus seen to be a merely serving priesthood both in relation to the active existential priesthood of Christ and the passive existential priesthood of believers. Priestly ministerial activity makes possible, that is, "facilitates" or "enables," a sacramentally enduring "making-present" for both. It has an essentially serving function. [2]

---

[2] Rahner, *Priestly Existence*, in *TI*, Vol. 3, London, 1967, pp. 249-250.

Nevertheless, in spite of these important qualifications, Rahner insists that the term priesthood is appropriate to describe the cultic ministerial power "in so far as (and only in so far as) the concept of priesthood denotes immediately only the power to posit the external cultic action and not the possibility of bringing about the corresponding inner disposition."[3] The cultic (sacrificial) ministerial activity of the priest is only meaningful as the visibility of the sacrifice of Christ. It is crucial and necessary that this activity be understood in the full concept of Rahner's sacramentology. This means that this sacramental activity is not a mere symbolic portrayal of an already existing purely "spiritual" presence, but "a liturgico-sacramental action which really makes present the salvation-mystery for us," a visibility and an externalization in which the invisibility and the inner reality of the graced activity of God first constitutes itself.

b. Priestly Ministry: A Definition

In light of these considerations, Rahner offers a definition of the priest — but he notes that his formulation does not depend on a strict boundary between the priest and the bishop. Hence, his definition is applicable to both.[4] He remarks that this approach of emphasizing the union between the priest and bishop is mirrored in the medieval theology which — although since Vatican II no longer supportable — denied a sacramental character to episcopal ordination.[5]

---

[3] Rahner, *Priestly Existence*, pp. 249-250; "bringing about", "effecting" = *Bewirkung.*

[4] Rahner, *Departure*, p. 36; ST, Bd. IX, pp. 370-371: "Bei dieser Begriffsbestimmung kommt es nun hier nicht auf eine Abgrenzung des Priestertums vom Bischofsamt an." The ET in *TI* fails to render this correctly. It states: "in defining this concept of the priesthood in these terms we are not seeking to set it apart from the episcopal office"(!). The ET in *Concilium* less inexactly —but wrongly— states: "In this definition we are not concerned with the distinction between priesthood and episcopacy" (*Concilium* 43, p. 85).

[5] Rahner, *Departure*, p. 36; ST, Bd. IX, p. 371: "Daß diese nicht ganz leicht vorzunehmen ist, zeigt der Umstand, daß die mittelalterliche Theologie der Bischofsweihe einen sakramentalen Charakter absprach, auch wenn man dies nach

Rahner's definition is: "The priest is s/he who, related to an at least potential community, preaches the word of God by mandate of the church (more exactly: "on behalf of the church") as a whole and therefore officially and in such a way that s/he is entrusted with the highest levels of sacramental intensity of this word."[6]

Rahner declares that any attempt to understand the essence of the "ministerial functions in the church which we designate as her official ministerial priesthood" must start at the church as one and whole. Only from this context can one understand the peculiarity of the functions which the presbyters in the church safeguard.

1° A Meaningful Complex of Tasks and Functions

The question, "what is it that the priest alone can do?" is not the most fundamental question, declares Rahner, for arriving at an understanding of the significance of the priestly ministerial office.[7] It is not possible to understand accurately the fundamental legitimacy and meaningfulness of a sacramental *Ordo* — that is, episcopal, presbyteral, and diaconal ministerial office — simply by saying that this or that in the church is possible only on condition that there is a corresponding ordination.

The approach that leads to a clearer understanding of priestly ministerial office is based upon a fundamental principle. It is that a sacramental sealing and confirmation of official ministerial and institutionalized functions in the church as society is meaningful and corresponds to the essence of the church. This principle

dem Zweiten Vatikanum so nicht mehr aufrechterhalten kann." The ET in *TI*, immediately following upon the mistranslation noted above in n. 4, inexactly translates:... "it is not altogether easy to separate the two entities one from another..." An even more serious error occurs in the ET of *Concilium* 43, p. 85: "That this distinction should not be underrated is clear from the fact that medieval theology attached (!) a sacramental character to the consecration of a bishop." (The fact that Rahner himself actually edited *Concilium* 43 is no guarantee that the ET renders his writing accurately.)

[6] Rahner, *Departure*, p. 36. The above rendering is the ET of *Concilium* 43, p. 85. The ET in *TI* is quite inexact and misleading.

[7] Rahner, *Theological Reflections on the Priestly Image of Today and Tomorrow* (hereafter *Priestly Image*) in *TI*, Vol. 12, London, 1974, p. 48.

remains valid notwithstanding the fact that "in themselves" such functions and tasks are able to be carried out without a prerequisite of ordination, and, in fact, actually are carried out.

What is important to understand in this approach is that what the priest concretely undertakes and accomplishes in the priestly ministerial office is a meaningful complex of tasks and functions. Their meaningfulness is based on the essence of the church itself. This particular complex, which is understood as a unity, legitimizes the priestly ministerial office itself, and is conferred in sacramental authorization upon a man or a woman. This united complex of tasks and functions are the contents of a special status in the church.

The principle upon which Rahner bases these reflections is that a sacramental ordination, in its essence and its meaningfulness, is not dependent on relating to something and making it holy — which otherwise in general would not happen. Rahner uses the example of the diaconate to exemplify his position. He comments that Cardinal Ottaviani, among others, has declared that there are no tasks or functions which a deacon carries out that could not also be done by a lay person. Rahner responds that in ordaining an individual a deacon, one is not giving to the deacon functions which one "would not otherwise possess and hence has not previously exercised."

According to Catholic teaching, there are three specific functions which are carried out exclusively by the priest: 1) the leadership of the eucharistic celebration; 2) the administration of the sacrament of penance; and 3) the anointing of the sick. The question that Rahner raises does not argue that these are and can remain "priestly" functions. Rather, is it justified for an individual to exercise these — and only these functions — and affirm that this appropriately constitutes a "profession" in the civic meaning of the term. Does the exercise of the complex of these three functions alone require that this be an individual's main occupation, either in an ecclesial or in a civic context?

Some functions that are in fact carried out by those in priestly ministerial office can be done by other persons as well. Clearly, the task of teaching, but also the task of being in charge, as well as the task of baptism do not require priestly ordination to be carried out. In regard to the tasks and functions that are exercised by those in priestly ministerial office, Rahner cautions that only by underscoring the fact that for the priestly ministerial office one understands a meaningful complex of tasks and functions can one hope to accurately express the relationship between those in priestly ministerial office and the other members of the church. For the "little which, according to the teaching of the Catholic faith, can be done only by ordained priests can hardly constitute the content and the function of a 'principal calling'" (more exactly: 'A principal ministerial-office profession').[8]

2° Proclaimer of the "Exhibitive" Word

Rahner cautions that his description of the priest in terms of a proclaimer of the word of God should not be misunderstood. He states that the word which is entrusted to the church, the word of witness, fundamentally has the character of "event", of being "exhibitive," of being "effective."[9] If one recognizes this in a fundamental way, it is appropriate and accurate to speak of the one proclaiming this word as a "prophet." But one must "understand by this word — for want of another — a human being whose word is not merely a talking about the word of God, but a human being in whose word the saving word of God itself encounters humankind."[10] When the church proclaims the word that God is victorious, that is, when it bears witness to this victory, the church is itself church in its most fundamental way.

The word which the church proclaims is event. Consequently church must be seen in a fundamental way as sacrament. As sacrament, the church does not communicate information in some objectified sense about the victory of God. Rather, the church is the sacrament of God's own self-communication. The victory of God is witnessed to as taking place in the church. As

---

[8] Rahner, *Priestly Image*, p. 46.
[9] Rahner, *Departure*, pp. 35-36.
[10] Rahner, *Priestly Existence*, p. 251.

with all human words, the event character of the word of witness of the church occurs in essentially different levels of intensity. That which is called a sacrament in the narrow, technical, theological sense of that term is the high point of the church's word of witness.

It is this element, that of the proclaimer of the exhibitive word, which Rahner sees as most essentially describing the uniqueness of the priestly ministerial office. This prophetic element "lays claim to the whole existence of the human being." This is so because the preaching of the Gospel not only requires the personal commitment of the messengers, but takes this in as an intrinsic element into itself. The proclamation of the Gospel is borne fundamentally by the proven witness that the grace which is preached is a reality in the one who is preaching.

In all of this, Rahner underlines the charismatic foundation of the proclamation of the Gospel: "the proclaiming of God's message is essentially a speaking in the Holy Spirit and in the power of God, and that all prophesying and teaching is a pneumatic charism."[11]

The priest is the one who is authorized for the service of the word in the church. One can recognize in this "definition" all the priestly tasks that are implied if one affirms the intrinsic multiple dimensions of this word: 1) its different levels of actualization and its exhibitive character; 2) its nature as not merely didactic but also as pointing to the prophetic; and 3) its character as promise.[12]

3° Unity of Word and Sacrament

Thus, an extremely important point is to see the fundamental unity between the proclaiming of the word and the administration of the sacraments. They possess a common mutual root, an ultimately united nature. This is a theme, in fact, that Rahner had already reflected on as early as 1942, though not with the same terminology that is used in his later writings. Possibly the criti-

---

[11] Rahner, *Priestly Existence*, p. 258.
[12] Rahner, *Priestly Image*, p. 51.

cism that is sometimes directed to Rahner in regard to his sacramentology may not recognize and take into account the full background and the fundamental unity that Rahner asserts between word and sacrament, one that is constitutive of the church itself.

The church is described by Rahner not only as the salvation-society, but also as the mediation of salvation. As the mediation of salvation, the church is the offer of salvation to humanity. As the salvation-society, the church appears as the acceptance of salvation. As the mediation of salvation, the church is the abiding actualization of God's exhibitive word of promise which is sent forth historically and is victorious eschatologically in Jesus Christ. This word Rahner describes as the *Grundwort*, the fundamental word. This *Grundwort* bears in its unity a four-fold character: 1) didactic; 2) sociologically juridical; 3) sacramental; and 4) prophetic.

4° Priest: Not Simply "Cult Official"

Consequently, based upon this fundamental unity of word and sacrament, Rahner concludes that the priest is not simply a "cult official." For from a theological perspective, the priest's whole existence as priest is one which must bear witness to the word of God, which is a word that effects salvation, an exhibitive word. "The priest is not merely ordained to say Mass, but as well for proclaiming the gospel in the name of the church, and this statement is not invalidated by the fact that it can be said that proclaiming the gospel can also be done without ordination."[13]

Rahner sees the priestly ministerial office able to be described as cultic-prophetic. In affirming this he says that one must recognize the instrinsic unity and the essential belonging-together of the cultic and the prophetic. The prophetic arises from the cultic, and it is the prophetic which alone fully realizes the cultic.

In itself, the cultic is not viewed by Rahner as existentially fundamental. He makes the personal observation that cultic activity is able to occupy only a small part of the whole life of an

---

[13] Rahner, *Priestly Image*, p. 49.

individual "even purely as regards time." But more significantly, he states that the cultic priestly ministerial office does not realize for the bearer of this office a reality that is different from that which can be realized by any other Christian. This cultic activity is fundamentally ordered to baptism and confirmation: "the cultic power of the priest as such is a new obligation to bring to development the old 'vocation' given by baptism and confirmation, not a new obligation to a new vocation of existential import not previously possessed."[14]

A theme that is in many ways the context as well as the exemplification of a focus on the cultic dimension is that of the relationship between the sacred and the profane, "before the temple." Rahner leaves no doubt as to his position: "There is no sacral sphere such as could be marked off as the holy temple and set apart from a profane and Godless world, as though it were only there, and not here, that the holy God of eternal life was waiting for us and was to be found."[15]

Consequently, Rahner declares that the bearer of the priestly ministerial office is not a holy representative of God who, with heavenly powers from God, faces an unholy people. The priest is rather the bearer of a particular and necessary function in a people whom God has made holy.

5° Priestly Ministerial Activity: A Fundamentally Serving Function

Both in regard to its cultic as well as its prophetic character, all priestly ministerial activity has an essentially serving function. This is manifested in a two-fold way both cultically and prophetically.

Cultic priestly ministerial activity has this serving function in relation to the active existential priesthood of Jesus Christ. This activity "does not merely 'symbolize' an absent reality, but really makes present something already made real by Christ. This cultic priestly ministerial activity also has a serving function in relation

[14] Rahner, *Priestly Existence*, p. 257.
[15] Rahner, *Priestly Image*, p. 44.

to the existential passive universal priesthood of believers. Through the mediation of sacramental activity believers are enabled to have co-participation and appropriation in the sacrifice of Christ. [16]

Similarly, prophetic priestly ministerial activity has an essential serving function in a two-fold way. In relation to Jesus Christ, the prophet, prophetic priestly ministerial activity continues to proclaim the message that is fundamentally Jesus' message, even recognizing that it is a charismatically transmitted message. In relation to believers, prophetic priestly ministerial activity is essentially a serving function as well. For the word of Christ can only be spoken in an area which from the start is enlightened by the light of the Logos.

Expressing himself in a summary fashion, Rahner declares that it is essential that those who are priests really understand themselves as servants of Christ, who "through the fathomless darkness of his death, has redeemed the world."[17]

6° Essentially Oriented to Community

And since the task of bearing witness to God's victory characterizes one's priestly existence, it means that the priestly ministerial office has a essential missionary character. Priestly ministerial office is essentially ordered to a community.[18]

Rahner also implies this relation to a community when he speaks of the character of the priest as "emissary." In fact Rahner sees the fundamental characteristic of the priestly ministerial office being based on this understanding of the priest as one who is sent, so that this being sent is again an element in the official cultic ministerial priesthood.[19]

One can also speak of this same reality by the term "prophet."

[16] Rahner, *Priestly Existence*, p. 253.

[17] Rahner, *Priestly Image*, p. 59.

[18] Rahner, *Departure*, pp. 36-37. The essential orientation to a community is an element of priestly ministerial office whether there is a relationship that is already in existence, or whether this is a task that is yet to be realized. It does not change essentially as regards the various sociological structuring that the community may have.

[19] Rahner, *Priestly Existence*, p. 262; "emissary" = *Sendling*.

Rahner indicates that it is essential to affirm that the concepts of the proclaiming of the word (prophet) and the administration of the sacraments (priest) in the context of Christianity "each now intrinsically qualifies and entails the other."[20] At the same time Rahner stresses that the joining together of these two concepts results in what he calls a certain deprivation of power, so that it gives rise to the question regarding the relationship between the universal priesthood and the official ministerial priesthood.

This fundamental relationship of the priest to a community must also be seen in a particularly important context. Today the church as "popular church" is changing to a church of professed believers — "who believe as an act of their own personal and free decision."[21]

The reality of community takes on a new character when seen in this perspective. And clearly it has consequences for the relationship between the one who bears priestly ministerial office and the community. The number of priests, their lifestyle, and the possibilities of their human existence will be first of all conditioned by the number, the economic possibilities, and the mentality of those who belong to such a church.

The academic formation of those who bear the priestly ministerial office in such faith communities is not required to be on a level that would simultaneously qualify one for a significant position in secular society. While affirming the importance for as many priests as possible to be "humanly and theologically highly educated," Rahner points out that the relationship between the priest and the community allows much greater variety in determining approporiate academic formation.

Another consequence that can result from the (potential) relationship of the priest to the faith community is in terms of the selection of a priest for a particular community. It is perfectly conceivable, notes Rahner, that a community of believers, no longer able to find a priest through the usual administrative

---

[20] Rahner, *Priestly Existence*, p. 243.
[21] Rahner, *Priestly Image*, p. 54.

means, finds and chooses from the midst of its "living" members a "senior person," who, with appropriate theological formation and human maturity, would be ordained by the bishop as "presbyter," as priest for this community.

Rahner considers that such individuals could be described as "part-time" priests. He is quick to add that he uses this term in its civic context, for theologically such a description is not possible. For Rahner it will always be important that there be bishops and priests "who also exercise the priesthod as 'main calling' in the civic sense." It is also possible that there be priests and bishops who also are so in a fully theological way, but who do not carry out their tasks as a civic profession. The rationale for such a possibility is not simply the growing shortage of priests, but the "positive opportunities and advantages" that it would have. Those who exercise such a "part-time" priesthood may be particularly suited to relate to non-territorial communities, with parishes continuing to be the "basic model" for priestly activity. The key factor here would be to determine a body of tasks which would be confirmed through sacramental ordination, and for which an individual would feel adequately prepared to carry out.

In support of this approach, Rahner points to the fact that this is presently an experience that is occurring with regard to the diaconate. Without diminishing in any way the full-time theological dimension of ordination to the diaconate, this does not require the individual to carry out on a full-time basis all the tasks for which one is ordained. The ordained deacon frequently continues to exercise a separate civic profession. Rahner considers the same approach to be valid with regard to the priestly ministerial office. He notes that history itself is witness to numerous concrete variations regarding how the priestly ministerial office has been shaped and continues to be shaped even today.

7° Vocational Sacrament: Relationship to Baptism-Confirmation

Ordination to ministerial office as well as matrimony are accurately seen as "vocational" or "profession" sacraments. Yet, the question arises as to why other vocations or professions are not viewed as sacraments. Rahner's response is that only when the assumption of a vocation or profession "determines the sphere of existential life of the Christian in a new and specifically proper way" is it accurate to speak of a new sacrament.[22]

Other "civic" professions — from a Christian, existential perspective — are "only inessential variations of the one Christian being and life which was already taken up with baptism and confirmation as characterizing sacraments, and not therefore new sacraments."[23]

A fundamental criterion to determine if a vocation-profession is a sacrament is whether it has, "within the public life of the church,... a specifically proper and special role" for this life. This special significance for the life of the church is present when such a vocation-profession is a special actualization, what Rahner calls a fundamental fulfillment, of the essence and life of the church itself. The reason why such an actualization of the church's essence and life is seen as a sacrament is because the church itself is the basic sacrament, the basic sign of grace in the world in general.

Within the context of these reflections, one can properly situate Rahner's assertion that the vocation-profession sacrament of "ordinary" Christian life is Baptism-Confirmation. He stresses the fundamental significance of Baptism-Confirmation by indicating that the monastic life is fundamentally only a living out of that "eschatological calling, which was taken up at baptism and which is lived also by other Christians." "Monastic life," declares Rahner, "is only a shaping of the baptismal life, and, therefore, in spite of its necessarily existential, but not necessarily *new* existential significance, *not* a new sacrament."[24]

[22] Rahner, *Priestly Existence*, pp. 254-255.

[23] Rahner, *Priestly Existence*, p. 255. In regard to Rahner's understanding of Baptism, see, Rahner, *Consecration in the Life and Reflection of the Church* (hereafter *Consecration*) in *TI*, Vol. 19, London, 1984, pp. 57-72, esp. pp. 58-60.

[24] Rahner, *Priestly Existence*, p. 256. The ET in *TI* does not clearly state Rahner's position by translating *Ausformung* = shaping as "development."

All of these reflections lead Rahner to conclude that the priestly ministerial office, seen as a vocation-profession sacrament — as Rahner likewise affirms of marriage — must have a fundamental, new existential significance. Only in this way is it theologically possible to recognize ministerial office itself as a sacrament.

8° Priestly Vocation and Priestly Profession

a) Relationship to civic society

In a presentation given over twenty-five years after his initial reflections on the priestly ministerial office as a vocation-profession, Rahner offers a sharper distinction between vocation and profession as it relates to priestly ministerial office.

He notes that a long tradition of 1500 years has been established in which the ministerial office and the task of the priest in the church has — for the world — also been a profession. Thus, over a long period of time, the priest has had within human society a function which "has been recognized and expected by that society itself."[25] In effect, it was taken for granted that the heavenly vocation to the priesthood was also an earthly profession. Rahner, however, concludes that as regards the essence of the priesthood this is not so in any necessary way.

A task that Rahner believes is an important one is to not presuppose that "the priesthood itself must be capable of being lived in such a way that it also constitutes our worldly profession". He finds support for his position by indicating that there are certainly vocations in the profane sphere which do not indicate at the outset a profession which society would want or expect as one's means of support. Examples of these vocations are "poets, philosophers, artists," and those who are prophets of a new understanding of existence. Thus, even in the profane sphere vocation and profession can already step on one another's toes, can have so strained a relationship with each other, that the impossibility on the part of society to institutionalize a vocation in a sociologically recognized profession can be a criterion of the authenticity of the vocation itself.

[25] Rahner, *Priestly Image*, p. 41.

Rahner does not repudiate, but joins with Paul the Apostle in declaring that one who serves at the altar may also live from the altar. Yet he insists that to really understand the priesthood from the center of one's existence, and to be able to undertake this priesthood in a ever-new way, it is imperative that one recognize that the priestly vocation does not necessarily have to be one's worldly profession.

Rahner not only insists that the priestly vocation is not identical to the priestly profession, he also recognizes that the two are inseparable from each other. This inseparability manifests itself particularly through a reality which the church as a whole experiences, and which does and must occur in regard to the priestly ministerial office: contradiction. In the relationship between church and world, the reality of contradiction is always present to some extent; for the "Christian faith always implies folly and scandal so far as the 'world' is concerned."

Rahner points out that as long as one believes in the permanent continuity of the church, one has no basis for denying the necessity of the permanent continuity of the priestly ministerial office. Consequently, this element of contradiction, inasmuch as the priestly ministerial office is inseparable from the church as a whole, necessarily is an experience of the priestly ministerial office. This contradiction is apparent in an opposition to the priestly profession on the part of secularized society. The same reality of contradiction is experienced by lay members of the church as well.[26]

What is strongly criticized by Rahner are particular expressions on the part of those in priestly ministerial office to the reality of contradiction which "cause scandal to the world," which are

[26] Rahner, *Priestly Image*, p. 52. See, also, Rahner's reflection concerning the relationship between the church —and, consequently, the priest— and the mystery of God, as the seeming "context" in which to understand the nature of this "contradiction." Rahner, *The Man with the Pierced Heart* (hereafter *Pierced Heart*) in *SL*, London, 1968, pp. 117-119, esp. p. 113: "Tomorrow's priest will be one whose calling is most difficult of all to justify in profane terms, because the priest's real success is always vanishing into the mystery of God and because the priest is not a psychotherapist dressed in the old-fashioned costume of a magician."

"unnecessary and regrettable," and which have nothing to do with the essence of the priesthood. The reality of contradiction must be recognized and not denied.

b) Priestly Holiness

More than ever before, the faith of the Christian — and consequently, the faith of the priest — is recognized as something that can never be assumed or taken for granted. Faith, notes Rahner, is meant to be difficult. There is no doubt that this is the case today. What must never be forgotten is that "faith is the impossible that grace alone makes possible."[27]

For the priest, therefore, there is — as ever — a clear call to holiness. The faith of a priest of today is the faith of a praying priest — one could almost say of a mystical contemplative priest — or it is nothing. This call to holiness arises from the priestly ministerial office itself. What Rahner describes as a basic law of one's life and of Christianity is this: the necessary unity of ministerial office and person.[28] The task that the priest must be dedicated to is achieving this oneness, a oneness that should be achieved. To this extent Rahner stresses that for the priest one's profession is one's life, and one's life is one's profession. The priest's life-task is an ever more intimate approximation between oneself and one's ministerial office. The importance of prayer for this task is based, declares Rahner, on the fact that only in prayer is the whole human being present in an unmediated way before God. On the other hand, to the extent that the priest does not strive for this oneness, this diastasis takes revenge in one's priestly ministerial profession. In as much as one's ministerial office exists, it becomes simply "sounding brass that nobody heeds. One's sacramental powers remain but in such a way that nobody wants them."

The theme of the holiness of the priest is a very significant one

[27] Rahner, *Today's Priest and his Faith* (hereafter *Today's Priest*) in *SL*, London, 1968, pp. 48-49.

[28] Rahner, *The Priestly Office and Personal Holiness* (hereafter *Priestly Holiness*) in *SL*, London, 1968, p. 104.

for Rahner. A book that focuses on this very specifically originated from a series of retreat conferences that Rahner gave in 1961 to a group of candidates preparing for ordination.[29]

9° Changeable Element of Priestly Ministerial Office

Bearing witness to the victory of God pertains to the enduring, unchangeable aspect of the priest. It must be distinguished from the changeable sociological aspects that necessarily make up the existence of the priest. This is true both in terms of ecclesial sociological realities and secular sociological realities. Rahner points out that the priest's tasks that are cultic may, sociologically speaking, provide for the priest's economic needs, but that in itself does not determine, theologically speaking, what is of a changeable or of an unchangeable nature of the priesthood. Thus, the concrete form in which the priest exercises the priestly task is extremely variable.

This realization means, in turn, that it is important and necessary to discern constantly what functions or tasks which are in practice carried out by those in priestly ministerial office may be carried out by those who hold other non-priestly ministerial offices in the church, without affecting in a detrimental way the nature of the priesthood.

Rahner believes that there has been an insufficient appreciation of what he calls the real possibilities that exist — of an internal as well as of an external nature — with regard to the changeable element of the ministerial office in general of the church. This, Rahner holds, is especially true with regard to the priestly ministerial office.

Consequently, he calls for a much more open spirit with respect to the possibilities of change for the priestly ministerial office. In order to truly safeguard the "abiding essence" of the priesthood, one must "maintain an attitude of freedom and openness towards a change in its external forms as and when this is demanded by the situation of the church today and in the future."[30]

To do this is a real challenge. There are many fears and

---

[29] Rahner, *The Priesthood*, New York, 1973.
[30] Rahner, *Priestly Image*, p. 59.

worries. Rahner cautions that one should be more fearful of a conservative tendency towards inertia, than fearful of too much courage for a new, creative shaping of the priestly ministerial office. Yet, because the present time so strongly questions the value of the church and even faith itself, in such an environment where ecclesial defeatism and much insecurity is found, the most important and needed response with regard to the priesthood is an unconditional hopeful faith in its existence and its task in the church today and tomorrow.

The future is not to be seen primarily as something which one simply endures. Rather the future must be shaped. Rahner offers a type of portrait — or perhaps more realistically, a sketch — of the priestly ministerial office. If the priest does not look on the ministerial office as a comfortable, established profession that supports all one's economic needs, then the priest has grasped the foolishness of the cross. If the priest is not a hireling but a shepherd, who hopes against hope; if the priest is one who declares her/his support for the scandal of the cross; if the priest has the patience to endure "historical situations which are impenetrable to one's gaze"; if the priest understands oneself as a servant of Christ who, "through the fathomless darkness of his death, has redeemed the world"; if one is ready, without emotionalism, to bear the stigmata of Christ in the plainness of one's gray daily life, then one is a priest. Then it is clear that it is God's grace alone which creates through one and through one's priesthood the future for this priesthood which the Lord of history and of the church has intended and which will be.

This same spirit of being ever open to a renewal of one's own priestly ministerial office is a theme which Rahner already stressed in 1932. Rahner clearly sees priestly ministerial office as a dynamic and not a static reality. Speaking on the occasion of a twenty-fifth anniversary of a man's priestly ordination, he affirmed that one only "has" the priestly profession so that one must ever anew acquire it with the remaining strength of one's heart, and — even more — with the grace of God.[31]

[31] Rahner, *No Regrets*, in *SL*, London, 1968, pp. 89-94. (Originally given in Freiburg 26 July 1932).

a) Indelible Character

Sometimes an appeal is made to the notion of the indelible character of the priesthood with the result that serious reflection about change does not take place. Modern exegesis, the history of dogma, church history, church sociology, and the needs of the present-day church, however, all compel one to a radical reflection on the changeable and the unchangeable element in the Catholic priesthood.

To begin from a consideration of an indelible character is not satisfactory. On the one hand, one simply identifies the indelible character with priestly existence and powers as such. There is no movement forward in gaining an understanding. On the other hand, the character can be understood in a more narrow fashion as an intrinsic "indestructible" spiritual sign. The result is that one is able to say very little theologically that is of any certainty. At most one can only offer "formal generalities." Rahner states that his fundamental understanding of the doctrine of the *character indelebilis* is that it is "concerned merely with the impossibility of ordination being repeated." He does not see the doctrine of the indelible character necessarily preventing the church from restricting "all priestly powers on justified grounds that any exercise of them would be not only unlawful but actually invalid."[32]

b) Confidently Accepting Priestly Ministerial Office

On the one hand, radical reflection upon priestly ministerial office would enable that which is truly unchangeable and of an enduring quality to be recognized with respect to priestly ministry. It would provide justification for an individual's acceptance of the priestly ministerial office with courage and confidence. On the other hand, such reflection would enable the church to concretize and divide its one ministerial office in such a way that it corresponds in an effective way to the church's commission and to the present-day situation.

---

[32] Rahner, *Priest*, p. 216.

c) Sociological Context

Rahner recognizes that the theological nature of the priestly ministerial office does indeed have the character of *ius divinum*, hence an unchangeable character, but the unchangeable never exists alone. It always takes root and expresses itself in and by means of the changeable. Consequently, the theological reality of the priesthood always occurs in the context of a historically determined concreteness. This is true in as much as the priestly ministerial office occurs in a changeable dimension within the sociological structure of the church itself. Because the church exists as a sociological reality in the world, the priestly ministerial office occurs in such a way that secular society accords it a certain role. Thus, the task is to ever-anew discern the unchangeable character of priestly ministerial office within the ever-changing character of that priestly ministerial office.

d) Praxis Required

This task, of necessity, cannot be recognized nor accomplished by means of theory alone. It demands praxis. Praxis affirms the need for learning from experience and experiment. The process of discernment can only occur through an encounter with priestly life.

10° Inadequate Starting Points

a) Sacramental Powers

Rahner concludes that it is not advantageous for determining the theological nature of priestly ministerial office to begin with an affirmation of the sacramental powers which pertain to the priest alone. This, Rahner believes, presupposes the hierarchical element and the traditional priestly service as something that is self-evident, but these are precisely what need to be the object of reflection.

b) Community Leadership Function or the Spiritual Element

Based on this realization, Rahner declares that it is equally disadvantageous to look exclusively to the community leadership function or exclusively to the spiritual element in order to determine theologically the priestly ministerial office.

c) Mediator

Similarly, to begin with the concept of mediator is not bene-
ficial for arriving at the theological nature of priestly ministerial
office. It raises more questions than it answers. For example,
from a sacramental perspective, Rahner points out that all sacramental mediation is only one particular manifestation — but a
manifestation that brings about that which is manifested — of the
graced relationship of human beings to God which extends
through all dimensions of human life — even without the mediation of the priestly ministerial office. Rahner stressed this point in
regard to the concept of mediator in relation to the priestly
ministerial office in 1942: "The sacramental salvation-reality of
Christ — in the Incarnation and the sacrifice of the cross — is the
one and only truly valid and final saving act of God in the world
and therefore the one and only final mediation between God and
human beings."[33]

11° Priestly Celibacy

In a conference in 1968, Rahner commented about priestly
celibacy. He states that he is very decisive in speaking out for the
continuation of celibacy even for the secular priest. He explains
himself by pointing out that, in his opinion, "any further seculari-
zation of the clergy would not be conducive to the health of the
church and of the priesthood." Rahner adds that the priest is
called to live and bear witness to his faith in eternal life — a life
which is not of this world — specifically through the renunciation
of the great good of marriage in accordance with the recommendation of scripture.

Rahner, nonetheless, recognizes that the question may still be
posed as to whether this holy burden should be imposed on all
groups of priests who will be formed in the future within the one
priesthood. His statement is an explicit acknowledgement that
there always will be great diversity within the priesthood. It is
quite possible, and may even be necessary, that there be groups
within this one priesthood who would not be celibate. Also

---

[33] Rahner, *Priestly Existence*, p. 247.

noteworthy is Rahner's emphasis on the collegial character of the priesthood in speaking of groups and not of an isolated individual. [34]

An open letter to "brother priests" on the topic of celibacy was published by Rahner a few months before the promulgation of the encyclical of Paul VI, *Sacerdotalis Caelibatus*. Declaring that he was not a prophet, there are four considerations that he wishes to present. 1) He does not wish or expect, the church to change the law of celibacy "for our Western regions". Rahner's qualification of speaking solely in regard to "Western regions" should be noted. 2) The church may nuance and improve its own implementation, orienting the education of its young theological students to a true attitude of celibacy, not through vague recommendations, but by concrete measures. 3) The church must be magnanimous in the praxis of dispensations, inasmuch as this pertains to church law — which is never the totality of the question. And 4) the Latin church may specifically confer the priesthood on men who are already married. Though this is not a common occurrence, Rahner notes that it may occur more often than previously, where there is a "mingling of all cultures and intellectual worlds." Even if such a reality were to take place as a normal course, such as is exemplified in the two-fold character of the diaconate, Rahner hopes that the church "will have the holy courage to continue requiring celibacy even of the secular clergy."[35]

---

[34] Rahner, *Priestly Image*, p. 59. See, in this regard, the further consideration made by Rahner in 1977: *Pastoral Ministries and Community Leadership* (hereafter *Pastoral Ministries*) in *TI*, Vol. 19, London, 1984, pp. 73-86.

[35] Rahner, *Episcopal Office*, p. 340. Rahner offers the "psychological" example that an African bishop may be viewed particularly in the context of tribal leadership. Historical presuppositions could be manifest in "one or another French bishop" such that there would be "something like a piece of the mentality of the ancien régime." And, although not mentioned by Rahner, sociological presuppositions could be very influential in situations, for example, where large numbers of immigrant peoples form part of the membership — already or newly :vangelized — of the local diocese.

c. Priest and Bishop

1° Theologically Dependent upon One Another

The theological definitions respectively of priest and of bishop are mutually determining for one another in many ways. Rahner points out that the renewed emphasis that the local bishop leads the diocese "in the name of Christ" and not in a merely delegated way could lead to an autocratic "episcopalism" — an unhappy exchange for "Roman Centralism." In central European countries there is very little danger of this happening. This is because in the context of the diaspora situation in which the church finds itself "bishops and priests are too dependent on one another in the crisis of neo-paganism." In other countries, however, the danger of "episcopalism" may be much greater. Both historical as well as psychological — and one may add, sociological — presuppositions undoubtedly have a strong influence on the style of leadership exercised by a local bishop.[36] Nevertheless, no matter what may be the local situation, Rahner states that it is essential to keep clearly in mind the "theologically correct relationship between the bishop and the presbyterium."

2° Presbyterium: *Iure Divino* a College for the Bishop

Rahner indicates that the relationship between the bishop and the presbyterium cannot be seen as identical to the relationship between the pope and the college of bishops. They cannot be seen as the same in such a way that what is seen as theologically constitutionally *iuris divini* with regard to the pope and college of bishops may simply be transferred in some univocal and mechanical way to the bishop and presbyterium. Nevertheless, there are two important considerations.

a) A model for Presbyterium and Bishop

First, the constitutional-theological structure of the church demands a unity of polarity, a unity of monarchical and collegial elements that are insolubly related to one another. Therefore, this

[36] Rahner, *The Celibacy of the Secular Priest Today: An Open Letter* in *SL*, London, 1968, pp. 149-172.

reality can be regarded as a model for the relationship of bishop and presbyterium.

b) Principle of Collegiality: No Individual Priestly Ministerial Office

Secondly, if the principle of collegiality applies to the relationship between bishop and presbyterium as a model, this has certain consequences. By priestly ordination, the priest enters into a college, the presbyterium. Rahner holds that the presbyterium is to be seen "fundamentally *iure divino* as a college for the bishop." In support of his position he states that "the New Testament and the primitive church do not actually show any knowledge of the single priest but only of the presbyterium."[37] He says that even though the three-fold level of the church's ministerial office is not actually defined, it nevertheless pertains to the "non-rescindable divine" constitutional law of the church.

The affirmation of this is not made in view of the priest as an individual. An enduring, unchangeable element in regard to the priestly ministerial office is essentially its collegiality. It is wrong to think that the priest — or the deacon — exists merely because the bishop needs help. If this were the case, it is conceivable that some bishop could decide that he does not need help, and do away with the priestly — and diaconal — ministerial offices without any problem. Rahner points out that such a situation could be realized very easily if one were to simply ordain all priests as bishops. The bishop, however, "does not ordain an individual, but surrounds himself with a college." The priest is not first of all ordained as someone who can "help" the bishop be present "everywhere." The priest is rather a helper to the bishop where the bishop is, not where the bishop is unable to be. Theologically, the presbyterium is not adding together and forming into a college the pastors of all the individual local worshipping communities. It is the other way around. All the pastors of the individual local worshipping communities are drawn from the one presbyterium that surrounds the bishop. In the early

[37] Rahner, *Episcopal Office*, pp. 340-341.

centuries of the church the theological and sociological reality of the presbyterium coincided in regard to place; the presbyterium gathered around the bishop locally.

c) Bishop and Presbyterium Exist Together

Even though the relationship between the bishop and the presbyterium must be such that the bishop has precedence over the presbyterium, the bishop has a moral duty to ensure that the members of the presbyterium who in practice "surround him" daily must truly be a representation of his full presbyterium. Such a moral obligation is called for not simply for purely pragmatic and psychological reasons, but for a truly constitutionally-theological reason: the acceptance of the polarity between the bishop and the presbyterium. This polarity is not an opposition, but a recognition of the fact that theologically bishop and presbyterium exist together — distinct and inseparable (to express it in terminology frequently — though in this instance, not explicitly — used by Rahner).

3° Each Local Community Needs a Leader from the Presbyterium

The recognition of the essential character of the presbyterium as *ius divinum* and not the individual bearer of the priestly ministerial office in the church leads to an important conclusion: "only when the priest is seen as always the member of the presbyterium does it become quite understandable why every head of a permanent, local altar-community of any size, that is, above all every parish priest is not a bishop."[38]

This understanding enables one to see the fundamental theological reality of the diocese. A failure to recognize the theological significance of the presbyterium can lead one to conclude that the diocese is merely a sociological necessity, a grasping together of individual local worshiping communities under their local leaders. A diocese is not merely "an administrative organization of many local communities, but a real spiritual entity." This

---

[38] Rahner, *Episcopal Office*, p. 342.

theological significance is lost if the bishop is seen to simply ordain a priest in order to send the priest away with her/his powers so that each one may be a priest for her/himself. Rather, the bishop gives to the members of the presbyterium — which permanently belongs to him — local individual tasks with the consequence that the bishop remains the "episcopal father of his whole diocese."

Rahner emphasizes that the mission entrusted to a member of the episcopal presbyterium that is seen as the normal and most frequent one is that of the local parish. However, members of the presbyterium may be called upon for other tasks as well. The territorial principle is the fundamental but not the only constitutive principle for the church. What must be avoided with regard to the centrality of the local parish is what Rahner calls a "romantic parochialism," which makes the pastor into a "little bishop." If the pastor is seen as a member of the episcopal presbyterium, then the pastor is clearly seen as the representative of the episcopal church then and there. The parish, emphasizes Rahner, "is not a diocese in miniature." Consequently, the pastor is not a little bishop.

4° Sacramental Powers: Bishop and Priest

a) Centrality of the Eucharist

The border between the sacramental power of the bishop on the one hand and the priest on the other is not so easy to delineate. The fundamental reason for this is that it is impossible to think of the bishop without the presbyterium. Although the bishop takes precedence over all the members of the presbyterium, possibly even a "subordinate member of this unity of bishop and presbyterium... can represent the bishop." This member is appointed as capable of this representation by sacramental ordination.

It is significant that the priest-member of the presbyterium carries out this task of representation in regard to the most central function of the bishop: the celebration of the Eucharist. It is the most central function of the bishop because it is in the Eucharist, which is the innermost mystery of the church, that this church "is made present most actually and most intensively" in the dimension of space and time.

b) Member of Presbyterium: To Represent the Head of the Presbyterium

If as a member of the presbyterium a priest can so represent the bishop in the eucharistic celebration, all other functions, *a fortiori*, are able to be exercised by the priest as representative of the bishop. The only function that a priest certainly cannot exercise is ordaining an individual a bishop — because the bishop always has precedence over the presbyterium. Rahner points out that it is not necessarily certain that a priest could not possibly administer priestly ordination, in a valid way. And there is no doubt that a priest can confirm. In actuality, a priest can be the bearer of all the jurisdictional power of a bishop.

c) Bishops no longer necessary?

Rahner concludes that abstractly speaking one could conceive of all the necessary ministerial offices of the church being administered by priests. One would need to have episcopal ordination only if there is a need of bishops. Bishops would not be needed if the bishop's functions which are "necessary for the salvation of Christians" could also be performed by an ordinary priest. Such a speculative possibility only shows how important and necessary it is to affirm that the bishop can never be seen without the presbyterium. It indicates that the border in terms of *ius divinum* "between priest and bishop is not so easy to draw as it is sometimes thought."

This appreciation of the mutually determining influence between bishop and priest indicates that the priest is not "a smaller 'recapitulation' of the bishop," but ultimately one who cannot be thought of apart from being a member of the bishop's presbyterium. This belonging together of priest and bishop is the fundamental reason why the priest's power as representative of the head of the presbyterium is in some way changeable. It is certainly important and necessary to recognize this changeableness that has occurred throughout some periods of church history, depending on the changing intention or purpose of the church with regard to priestly ordination.

5° Priestly Ministerial Office Changeable in Relation to Episcopal Ministerial Office

Rahner makes the significant assertion that notwithstanding that the church's ministerial office is fundamentally *one*, a partial participation in the ministerial office of a society is changeable from the nature of such participation and the historical situations without the result that the essence of the one ministerial office is changed. Rahner holds that this legitimately applies to the church's one ministerial office which is *iuris divini* and its threefold division. For example, it could be declared that under no circumstances is a priest capable of conferring priestly ordination. This would not mean that this always has been this way nor that it always must stay this way. Such an understanding would aid in diminishing or eliminating many difficulties arising about the church's ministerial office in the context of the first periods of the church. By the church's determining — sometimes very implicitly — the scope of the powers that are conferred by means of priestly ordination, the difference between the priesthood and the episcopal ministerial office varies.

d. Women and Priesthood?

The Sacred Congregation for the Doctrine of the Faith, with the approbation of Paul VI, published 15 October 1976, a *Declaration on the Question of the Admission of Women to the Ministerial Priesthood*. Rahner offers some theological reflections concerning the declaration.[39] In fact, he indicates that he is reflecting only on the theological aspects of this question, and even more specifically on the theological aspect of this particular declaration. Nevertheless, the considerations that Rahner presents do offer a view that is not restricted to the declaration itself. For he chooses to center on the question: "whether it is certain that the

[39] Rahner, *Women and the Priesthood* (hereafter *Women*) in *TI*, Vol. 20, London, 1981, pp. 35-47.

Christian revelation in its unchangeable substance excludes women from the priestly ministerial office in the Catholic church."

In regard to the declaration itself, Rahner notes that it carries a certain weight simply because of its origin from a Roman Congregation. It cannot be seen as identical to what an individual theologian may say. However, even though it enjoys papal approbation, the declaration "is not a definitive decision; it is in principle reformable and it can be erroneous." Recognizing that the declaration is an authentic but not a defined teaching, Rahner stresses that the fundamental question is whether the declaration is making an appeal "to a 'divine' or a merely human tradition." As a theologian he has a serious obligation to critically examine this declaration because of the possibility that it is erroneous. He notes that this attitude has not been displayed as courageously as it should have been over the last one hundred and fifty years — without taking into account the situation of earlier centuries. The theologian has an indispensable role to play in helping to assure the effectiveness of the proclamation of the church. Naturally, the theologian must carry out this responsibility with respect.[40]

The principal argument of the declaration, as Rahner reads it, is that the praxis of Jesus and the apostles knows of no ordination of women as priests, and that this reality is not one that is "historically and sociologically conditioned: that is, it holds for all times and must be respected faithfully by the church at all times."

A fundamental premise for Rahner is that a practical maxim of bahavior can be culturally and sociologically conditioned, and that precisely through a change of the cultural and sociological situation this practical maxim of behavior itself becomes change-

[40] Rahner, *Women*, pp. 38-39. In regard to this important function of the theologian, see, Rahner, *Reflections on Methodology in Theology*, in *TI*, Vol. 2, London, 1974, pp. 81-83. Respect is shown by a theologian — in regard to this declaration — who 1) attempts to impartially appreciate the reasons presented; 2) respects the consequent practice of the church as binding for oneself; 3) sees reinforced by this declaration the conclusion that there is not yet a general change of awareness with regard to legitimate opportunities for women in the church.

able and specifically is changed. Such an understanding is not threatened by the fact that in the earlier situation, such a practical maxim of behavior was not simply permitted but may have been obligatory. Rahner offers some examples of history that exemplify this reality.[41] Hence, because the church exists as a sociological reality, it cannot but help to be formed by and to form aspects of that cultural sociological reality that can never be done away with. The curious consequence is that the church, because of its sociological character, can actually slow down sociological and cultural change — change that would better realize the values that the church proclaims.

Consequently, Rahner asserts that it was both inconceivable and impossible at the time of Jesus or Paul to set up any female leaders of community or presiders of the eucharistic celebration. Jesus or Paul could not have been expected to see explicitly any contradiction between an affirmation of the fundamental dignity of human beings and this practical maxim of behavior. With all of this in mind, Rahner concludes that the burden of proof lies with the declaration to give evidence supporting the contention that women were not excluded because of the sociological and cultural situation of the time.

Additional criticisms voiced by Rahner are these: The declaration moves from the concept of apostle and the twelve to that of priest and bishop in a too simple and unnuanced way. The complexity of the "origins, structure, and organization of the primitive church" is not dealt with in a satisfactory way. A serious failure in the declaration is that it does not address the important issues of the "concrete emergence of the church and its origin from Jesus. An even more fundamental criticism is that the declaration does not work from "a clear and comprehensive concept" of the priestly ministerial office. In the fifth and sixth sections of the declaration, the particular tasks of the priest are

---

[41] Rahner, *Women*, p. 42. The examples that Rahner gives are: 1) the institution of slavery at the time of the first Christian century; 2) polygamy in the Old Testament; 3) the laws of war in the Old Testament; and 4) the ecclesial prohibition of usury up to the eighteenth century.

more or less restricted "to the sacramental power of consecration." This dangerously narrow understanding of the priestly
ministerial office gives rise to very serious dogmatic and especially
pastoral misgivings. The question must be posed not in terms of
sacramental powers, but rather from the perspective of community leadership. The argument that a person with a mandate of
Christ who is — in this way and not otherwise — "*in persona
Christi*," must represent Christ specifically in Christ's maleness is
not comprehensible.

Rahner's basic conclusion is that the attitude of Jesus and his
apostles is sufficiently clarified from the context of the sociological and cultural milieu of that time. Consequently, their behavior
must not possess a normative significance for all time — specifically if and inasmuch as this sociological and culutral milieu
essentially changes. Rahner underscores his conclusion in spite of
the fact that this practical maxim of behavior has persisted for so
long and with such little opposition.[42]

Ultimately, the discussion must continue, but discussion alone
is not sufficient. Historical change will decisively come about
through praxis — a praxis of life and of history that occurs in
freedom, action, and decision. The church must have the courage
to bring about the "historical change which is part of the fidelity
which the church owes to its Lord." His admonition that one
must work and struggle for this change with patience, is balanced
by his deep conviction that "time passes" and one cannot wait
for a hundred years for a solution to this question without real
detriment to the church. The urgency of the matter is clear.

---

[42] Rahner, *Women*, pp. 44-45. In regard to a general presentation of the
historical material to be considered on this topic, Rahner refers to H. van der
Meer, *Women Priests in the Catholic Church? A Theological-Historical Investigation*, Philadelphia, 1973.

2. Diaconal Ministerial Office

a. Fundamental Starting Points

1° Forming Community

One of the tasks of the ministerial office of the church is to form and build community. This task cannot be understood as one that exists next to the task of the mediating of salvation to the individual. Rather, the formation of community makes explicit the fact that salvation for human beings takes place in both the uniquely individual as well as the sociological-community dimension. Because the task of building community requires a particular type of knowledge and of skills, it follows that it is a task that is and can be carried out specifically only by some of those who hold ministerial office in the church.

Salvation for the individual must be lived out in a particular ecclesial and sociological position. This implies that an individual is integrated into a community. In times past, the church could take for granted that an individual was socially integrated into secular society. Consequently, the church did not have to concern itself with the necessary presuppositions for the formation of a human society. The church simply built upon it. But this is no longer the case.

2° Human Brokenness

Today, the society that the individual encounters, notes Rahner, is a society that exemplifies disintegration. There are not only the poor and the oppressed, but also many others who are not truly integrated into society: those who are lonely, those who have been cast aside by society, and those young who have not yet been integrated into society. While the task of integrating all individuals into society is essentially a human task, it is one that necessarily involves the church because the church exists as a tangible, historical, sociological reality. Indeed, the "integration of the individual at the human level into the human community and society is the necessary prior condition for the forming of an ecclesiastical community".[43]

---

[43] Rahner, *On the Diaconate*, in *TI*, vol. 12, London, 1974, p. 73.

It is this task that Rahner says surely can be described as a diaconal task. It is a task of the ministerial office of the church as such. However, since it requires a particular competency to carry it out, Rahner concludes that the church must make a special division of the one ministerial office which can specifically be called diaconal.

b. New Needs: Not a Repetition of History

1° Vatican II: Three Perspectives

The Second Vatican Council considered the question of the diaconal ministerial office, and Rahner himself was a significant participant in the discussion. The publication in 1962 of the work *Diaconia in Christo*, co-edited by Rahner and Vorgrimler, had a singular influence. Nevertheless, only three years — almost to the day — after the closing of the Council, Rahner declared that the motivation which influenced the Council to approve a restoration of the diaconate was insufficient for defining the "meaning and the content of the diaconate of the future."[44]

Three texts in Vatican II treat the topic of the diaconate. The motivation in favor of a restoration of the diaconate is varied in each of the three. In *Lumen gentium* the emphasis is on the importance of specific functions, particularly as seen on the basis of the New Testament. In *Orientalium ecclesiarum*, the focus is on the ancient order of the ordination sacrament. In *Ad gentes*, the stress is on the fact that diaconal service is already being carried out in practice.[45]

Rahner himself states that during the days of the Council, his argument was that since the diaconate already exists anonymously in the church, it is meaningful that it be sacramentally

[44] Rahner, *Diaconate*, p. 67.
[45] Rahner, *Diaconate*, p. 67, esp. n. 6. The reference to *LG* is n. 29, to *Orientalium ecclesiarum* (hereafter *OE*) n. 17, and *AG*, n. 16. Rahner specifically studies these three texts in regard to the diaconate: see, Rahner, *The Teaching of the Second Vatican Council on the Diaconate* (hereafter *Teaching on Diaconate*) in *TI*, Vol. 10, London, 1973, pp. 222-232; first presented at a conference in Rome 22-24 October 1965.

conferred upon those who are exercising it. This approach, though not unjustified even today, is "no longer adequate." He reasons that this approach "was influenced too much by the model of the earlier forms of the diaconate."

2° New Forms

It is the present which must influence the development of the diaconal ministerial office. An essential element is the "concrete situation of the church." This is important to emphasize because "whatever authentic basis we find for instituting the diaconate in the future... must be such that it does not in any sense depend upon the postulate that this concrete form of the diaconate as conceived of in the present must have been in existence all along and of necessity, and must continue to exist for all time."[46]

In addition, the diaconal ministerial office should not be seen in an univocal way. Just as with the priestly ministerial office, there can be a great deal of diversity as to how the diaconal ministerial office is shaped and formed.

As to the actual process of the formation of the diaconal ministerial office, Rahner underscores the fact that "practical and concrete experimentation" is absolutely essential. Pure theological reflection cannot adequately produce the concrete decisions that must be made. Still, in the process of experimentation, Rahner calls for level-headedness as well as prudence, which can only occur by means of theological reflection.

Through a wide variety of experimentation, a single theological essence will be able to be recognized which is common to each concrete diaconal ministerial office. In many ways, these will almost be forced upon the church as it responds to the needs that it encounters in today's situation.

c. Relationship to Priestly and Episcopal Ministerial Office

1° A New Theology of the Priestly Ministerial Office
There is a clear and very direct relationship between the

---

[46] Rahner, *Diaconate*, p. 70.

priestly ministerial office and the impetus to develop the diaconal ministerial office. There are two factors which, Rahner believes, the Council did not even foresee with regard to the development of the diaconate.

First, there are the conclusions that have been reached regarding a New Testament theology of ministerial office and its implications for understanding priestly ministerial office. These conclusions, in Rahner's view, affirm that in terms of the New Testament there is a ministerial office of the church, and it is fundamentally one. This one ministerial office can be divided into many functions "according to the concrete needs of any given community." So, while it is accepted that the three terms bishop, presbyter, and deacon, all occur in the New Testament, there is no "unambiguous delimitation" of each of these three terms. Nor is it possible to recognize clear limits between this one ministerial office of the church and other charisms which are not necessarily to be regarded as having a specific institutional and official ministerial character.

Secondly, there are the ecclesial and the secular sociological situations in which the priestly ministerial office exists. On the one hand, the priest's setting in the framework of secular society is no longer the same as in the past. Questions are raised, for example, as to whether the priest shall not exercise a secular profession that would, among other things, provide for economic support.

At the same time, due to a serious shortage of priests today, some are led to consider the possibility of individuals carrying out the tasks of the priestly ministerial office on a "part-time" basis — as seen from the perspective of secular society — while exercising a "full-time" secular profession. Within the church itself, Rahner notes that those in the priestly ministerial office have "gathered to themselves and exercised functions in the church which are both very intensive and numerous" but which need not be exercised precisely by priests.

Theologically, as well as practically, all of this has an impact on the diaconate as well. It underscores the fact that while the ministerial office in the church is ultimately one, in regard to its functions and its division into different ministerial offices, there is much more elasticity, more flexibility, and more fluidity than has been imagined in the last few centuries. Consequently, one can impartially consider more exactly both the content as well as the mutual demarcation of the three classic ministerial offices. This opens the way for a more profound and a specifically new, creative theology of the diaconate.

Similar to Rahner's vision with regard to the priestly ministerial functions, it is important to recognize a complex of functions that can be conferred together. In this way, "what a deacon is and what a deacon should be in the future" is an open question. The framework of this openness is formed by three "invariable" factors with regard to the diaconal ministerial office: 1) the deacon receives the ministerial office with its powers and duties; 2) the conferring of the diaconal ministerial office by the bishop has a sacramental character; that is, it must be conferred in a public sacramental act that expresses the wide scope of the conferral of this ministerial office; 3) the deacon does not have the normal power of leadership of an eucharistic celebration, for though in itself this power of leadership does not define completely the priestly ministerial office, it is, nevertheless, a power that is proper to the priestly ministerial office.

2° A Share in the Episcopal Ministerial Office

The church has a fundamental service orientation and task on behalf of all people. There is, consequently, what Rahner describes as a "universal Christian *diakonia*" for which all members of the church have a responsibility. There is also a special *diakonia* of ministerial office itself. For on the one hand, ministerial office can only be understood as a power, duty, and capability for service to other Christians and all human beings. On the other hand, since the church is a sociological and institutional society, there is a need for a special ministerial office which participates in the universal *diakonia* by exercising special functions and having necessarily the corresponding power to carry them out.

Inasmuch as a bishop gives a share of the ministerial office of loving service to a particular human being, and, consistent with that service empowers one to the service of the bread of life —the Eucharist and the word of God— and to other services in a permanent ministerial office in sacramental ordination, the bishop thus establishes the ministerial office of a deacon.

3° Negative Limits

The diaconal ministerial office can also be more clearly seen in contrast to the priestly and episcopal ministerial offices. There are four aspects in particular that Rahner notes.

a) Diaconate: Not a Leadership Function

The function of leadership is a specific function of the priestly and episcopal ministerial office. Certainly it is possible for a deacon — for example, where there is a shortage of priests — to be given such leadership functions. In this case, the deacon is exercising leadership in a subsidiary way, which is possible through the deacon's belonging to the one ministerial office.

b) Deacon: Not a Substitute nor Mediator for Laity

The universal diaconate is not replaced by the diaconal ministerial office. The mission and the duty of the laity cannot be transferred to the deacon. Nor can the deacon be seen to exercise in any sense the role of mediation between clergy and laity. Theologically, the deacon belongs to the church's one ministerial office. Even more fundamentally, there is in principle no need for such mediation, although it can happen that, in an ecclesial sociological context, the deacon does exercise such a function in a subsidiary way.

c) Diaconate: Not Rooted in Cultic Powers

The particular cultic-liturgical actions that are exercised by the deacon, can, with proper authorization, be carried out by any lay person in the church. Rahner insists that these specific cultic activities are not so important in themselves to constitute a specific ministerial office in the church. Such functions, he states, should be left with lay persons. Even the grouped complex of cultic functions entrusted to the deacon does not fundamentally express the nature of the diaconal ministerial office.

d) Diaconal Functions Not Removed from Priest and Bishop

Finally, the fact that the deacon manifests and exercises in a particular way the diaconal dimension of the one ministerial office of the church does not permit priest or bishop to give up responsibility for diaconal service in and through their own participation in the one ministerial office of the church. The fundamental reason for the division of the ministerial office is not to split up functions into totally separate ones. Rather, it is based on the fact that no one bearer of ministerial office can carry out everything that is required by that ministerial office all alone.

d. Diaconate and Sacramentology

1° Sacramental Foundation of Diaconal Ministerial Office

The diaconal ministerial office of the church can only be carried out in a way that corresponds to its very essence, if it is carried out in faith, hope, and love. So it is that sacramental grace is mediated through a rite of appointing an individual to a ministerial office in the church. What this expresses is that the church's ministerial office in its completeness can never fully and definitively be separated from its endowment with the Spirit. The ministerial office of the church necessarily manifests itself in the sociological and historical dimension. It cannot be otherwise. Any appointment to a ministerial office of the church is necessarily always the offer and promise of grace. For it is grace which alone makes the carrying out of a ministerial office effective in the full ecclesial sense.[47]

a) Not a "point" of grace in time

The bearer of a ministerial office is "made holy" inasmuch as

---

[47] Rahner, *Diaconate*, pp. 77-78. See, also, Rahner's considerations concerning the sacramentality involved with women deaconesses in the early church: Rahner, *Consecration*, p. 69: "It is not furthermore ruled out historically that one can accord a sacramental character to the early church ordination of deaconesses."

that person is enabled not to seek one's own salvation in an "egoistical" way, but truly to serve one's neighbor in the church. Consequently, the appointment to a ministerial office that takes place through sacramental ordination does not mean that God's grace is restricted solely to that one point of time. Rather, it signifies the promise of God to support in the individual's life the complete conduct of the ministerial office of the one ordained. Thus, the grace of God actualizes itself ever anew in the life of the deacon.

b) Diaconal sacramental character

The appointment to the diaconal ministerial office of the church is an appointment which is permanent, and hence irrevocable. Therefore the promise of grace on God's part is also permanent. This permanency essentially founds the understanding of the concept of sacramental character (*character indelibilis*) that one meets in tradition — specifically in the Council of Trent. It would be inexact and misleading to understand by diaconal sacramental character anything other than the permanency of the specific task of service to which one is appointed in ministerial office, and the permanency of the office of grace on the part of God.

2° Relationship in General between Grace and Sacrament

An understanding of diaconal ministerial office has to be situated within a general understanding of the relationship between grace and sacrament. The most fundamental misconception is to regard sacraments as the only experience of grace. Such a position, stresses Rahner, is false. He notes that an individual who is seeking God in faith, hope, and love is, by that fact, justified — before receiving the baptism of water. Similarly, in most cases, the repentant sinner who comes to the sacrament of penance comes as one whose sins have already been forgiven.

The two factors which both justify and require the reality of sacrament are: 1) the essence of the human being as a bodily person; and 2) the "incarnational" dynamism of grace itself; for grace is always the grace of Christ, which is able to achieve its full effectiveness only in the historical tangibility of space and time.[48]

3° Application to Diaconal Ministerial Office

From the context of his sacramentology, Rahner emphasizes that those who are carrying out truly diaconal ministerial tasks, but are doing so as lay members of the church, are promised and receive grace for service of neighbor, just as grace is manifested and communicated in sacramental ways in the sacrament of diaconate. He stresses this point "for the 'consolation' of those who, in virtue of the functions which they do *de facto* exercise in the church, are striving to attain to the diaconate as a sacrament, but have not yet had it conferred upon them through the imposition of hands." Although he does not explicitly says so, it would seem reasonable to conclude that this situation would exist for both men and women.

At the same time, however, the fact that the service of a lay person cannot, of necessity, be devoid of grace, does not do away with the meaningfulness and the relative necessity of the sacramental diaconate. On the contrary, the pre-sacramental and the extra-sacramental grace presses — because of its incarnational dynamic — for its sociological and bodily visibility in the church, for its sacramental manifestation in the church. This is so much the case that, conversely, its embodiment is the effective sign that brings about the grace itself. Thus, in the church diaconal functions that are being carried out tend toward a recognition and a conferral which can be called a particular sacrament of appointment to ministerial office.

3. Other Sharing in the One Ministerial Office

a. New Ministerial Office

In an article first published in 1982, Rahner contends that the episcopal, priestly, and diaconal ministerial offices of the church

[48] Rahner, *Diaconate*, p. 79.

are not absolutely the only ministerial offices. There are other functions — present in the church or conceivable — which are similar or analogous to the three classic ministerial offices.[49]

There are functions — Rahner mentions, for instance, one whose profession is a religion teacher — that an individual does and can exercise in the church which participate in the official ministerial task of the church with respect to the Christian people. These functions are not to be seen ultimately as merely secular support services for the benefit of the official ministerial priesthood. Rather, these are functions which at least in an analogous way share in the mission and task of the sacred ministerial office in the church as it is ultimately one. One must recognize that an individual who is carrying out such a function in the church "is surely not simply a lay person in the church in the same way as an attorney might be; nor does he or she have the same function in the church as the person who keeps the church clean for the pastor." Ultimately, such tasks that are of real significance for the church are carried out as a response to a concrete situation. This means that the boundaries of such other ministerial offices and function can be fluid with respect to the specifically missionary mission and task of all Christians.

Rahner believes that the particularity of the task and function in the church that is being carried out by a lay member of the church must not be minimized. He states, for example, that a married theology professor who carries out a task in the church of forming others as proclaimers of divine revelation should not insist on saying: "I am a lay person and want to be a lay person." There is a wide degree of difference in how each member of the church can and actually does participate in the church's ministerial office. In this regard, the distinction between clergy and laity is not so easy to ascertain.

---

[49] Rahner, *New Offices and Ministries in the Church*, in K. Lehmann, A. Raffelt (eds.) *The Practice of Faith*, London, 1985, pp. 169-171.

b. Participation in the Sacramentality of the Three Classic Ministerial Offices

In his nuanced manner, Rahner declares that one can ask in an impartial way whether such new ministerial offices and functions participate in the sacramentality of the church's one ministerial office. In support of an affirmative answer, he points to the fact that historically —with Thomas Aquinas and many medieval theologians— the episcopal ministerial office —as episcopal— was not seen to participate in the sacramentality of the church's ministerial office. However, with that view explicitly rejected by Vatican II, the sacramentality of the episcopal ministerial office is not established, but simply recognized. Thus, the same can occur in the case of other ministerial offices in the church. There may be anonymous ministerial offices in the church today whose spirituality — and sacramentality — is waiting to be recognized. And there can also be new ministerial offices formed which can participate in the sacramentality of the church's one ministerial office.

But Rahner's position is very emphatic with regard to some cases of those who are carrying out tasks that are similar or identical to that of the priest or deacon. Thus, if there are or must be pastoral assistants today who are permanent official ministerial leaders of a community that has no priest, then one should, in God's name, ordain them priests. Rahner's reason is that through ordination one does not receive something which one otherwise did not have; but, rather, that which is already present in an individual is fixed sacramentally and tangibly in the dimension of the church's ministerial office. Rahner vigorously defends his approach by pointing to the similar situation of an individual who is living a life with God but has never been baptized. The reason for the baptism, declares Rahner, is so that the life the person is already living manifests itself expressly in the dimension of the sociological and historical tangibility of the church.[50]

[50] Rahner, *The Spirituality of the Priest in Light of his Office*, in *TI*, vol. 19, London, 1984, p. 127.

c. Pastoral Assistants (in Priestless Communities) and Sacramentology

The ministerial office of pastoral assistants is one which has emerged in Central Europe as a result of praxis. The fundamental reasons that have led to the emergence of pastoral assistants are two-fold: 1) too few priests willing to accept the obligation of celibacy; 2) the reality of priestless communities for which a regular eucharistic celebration and the administration of the sacraments is no longer ensured. [51]

Pastoral assistants have a complete theological training. The episcopal ministerial church, in its pastoral crisis, assigns to these theologically trained laity those tasks and powers for which a priestless community has need, but which are not certainly bound to sacramental ordination. Theologically this presents problems. First, the priest tends to be described and delineated only in terms of the two sacramental powers of presiding at Eucharist and administering the sacrament of penance. This is an unacceptable idea of the priest, one that is narrowly ritualistic, viewing the priest in a purely cultic way. Secondly, from the position of the pastoral assistant, if the tasks and functions of being appointed permanently to lead a community are indeed more important and more comprehensive than that of the deacon, then should not the permanent appointment of a pastoral assistant be recognized as sacramental.

The fundamental question, as Rahner sees it, is: "If the church, which is the basic sacrament confers a permanent ministerial office, which is of very considerable importance for its reality, can it simultaneously not want such a ministerial office to participate

---

[51] Rahner, *Pastoral Ministries*, p. 77. See, also, Rahner, *Epilogue*, in W. Bühlmann, *The Church of the Future*, New York, 1986, pp. 185-197. "If, for example, the church in the future still insists on celibacy, very far-reaching changes will be called for, not all of which have been thought out by Rome, much less acted upon, but which will inevitably come, if the church is not to shrivel into a small sect. With a small body of celibate clergymen, the laity will necessarily achieve greater self-reliance, influence, and importance than it has now. Lay persons will become, from below, in basic communities, the agents of self-realization of the church" (p. 197).

in the promise which God gives to the church?" The only way out of this theological dilemma is to recognize the precondition which allowed the emergence of pastoral assistants: the law of celibacy. Rahner concludes that: "without the law of celibacy, pastoral assistants in fact and in practice would become priests."

In even stronger language, Rahner asks why this schizophrenia is allowed to proliferate. The result will be a "tacit Protestantization" of the church, merely because the church continues to link priesthood with celibacy and a certain academic training. He declares how incomprehensible it is that from the time of Pius X to the present, "the requirements for receiving Holy Communion have been reduced to a minimum, while requirements for presiding at the eucharistic celebration have been extended to what might be called a European maximum, which at least in a great part of today's world seems unreal."[52]

d. "Merely" Commissioning to Ministerial Tasks

Rahner finds a great urgency in recognizing and affirming the sacramental dimension of the significant and important ministerial tasks that are carried out by non-ordained members of the church. The urgency that he feels is this: "if the present development continues, the greater part of the administration of the church's one ministerial office will be safeguarded by those who do this "merely" on the basis of a church commissioning without "ordination". Those who share in the church's one ministerial office in significant ways must have that participation confirmed as to its full meaning. Not to do so is to diminish the church itself as the basic sacrament.

Courage must be employed to see whether other determined and limited official ministerial powers in the church can be given sacramentally in new forms of the one *Ordo* by means of a particular "ordination". This must be done if one is to avoid the above-mentioned laicization of the church, which would result if

---

[52] Rahner, *Consecration in the Life and Reflection of the Church,* in *TI*, vol. 19, London, 1984, p. 71.

the church continues to give precedence to having community leaders who accept the requirement of celibacy over the right of the community to have a sacramentally ordained leader.

e. Clergy and Laity: A Constantly Shifting Boundary

Rahner stresses that holiness is the foundation of all ministerial offices in the church. Within the one church all are made holy in the center of their existence. But, he says, there is certainly a distinction that is real — though of a secondary sort — between a lay person and a cleric. There is a special consecratedness in the dimension of sacramental sign and of a particular commissioning to a ministerial office which does not pertain to everyone in the church. It is more important, however, to recognize that where the particular boundary between clergy and laity lies, and where — in the light of a theologically clarified understanding of the church's ministerial office — it ought to lie, are questions for which the answer is still — for a long time now not clear in every respect. They are questions for which an unchangeable answer can never be found. Rather, they are questions that are always situated in the sociological, historical, and tangible life of the church. That is where the answers must be sought.

CONCLUSION

The one ministerial office of the Church exists because the Church exists as the historical, sociological and tangible continuity of Jesus Christ. Apart from the Church, ministerial office has no meaning. Apart from Jesus Christ, the Church has no meaning.

The theology of Karl Rahner stresses the fundamental desire and act on the part of God to make all things one. This does not mean abolishing the multiplicity that constitutes the finite world. It is the world as finite that God chooses to love and with which God chooses to be united.

Rahner's specific theology of the Church's ministerial office forms a part of his overall theology. He evidences a profound understanding of the complexities of history, but he keeps his eyes fixed on the ever-new horizon that is history in the making. He convincingly emphasizes the responsibility that human beings have today for shaping and fashioning that history so that God's purpose is fully manifested and fully realized.

In today's Roman Catholic Church, there is a great deal of interest with regard to the life of the Church. There are members of the Church who are expressing a readiness to share more explicitly, more significantly, in the Church's one witness of salvation to the world. This demands a spirit of cooperation and collaboration among all who form the one Church.

The Spirit of Jesus Christ is the source of the Church's life. The movements of this one Spirit must be discerned with wisdom and understanding, with faith and hope. Those who already share explicitly in the Church's one ministerial office particularly bear that responsibility. They are perhaps most conscious of the need to build up and realize the oneness that is rooted in the one Lord, the one faith, and the one baptism. This oneness can only be accomplished through the mulitplicity of many tasks and functions — and, ultimately, through many individuals. This multiplicity is not simply of practical value. Theologically it manifests the way God chooses to make all things one.

Present pastoral needs must form an essential part of how the Church exists. There are many questions which must be faced in regard to ministerial office if the Church will as fully as possible manifest the dynamism of God's Spirit. It is not an easy task. It is a task that brings together God and human beings in a most intense way. This study has reflected on this reality in the hope that it will be realized in history — and so not immediately and once and for all, but with courage, with confidence, and with trust in God's victorious love.